MW00776582

GLUTEN FREE

COOKBOOK

*365 DAYS OF UNBELIEVABLY EASY NO-GLUTEN
RECIPES TO BEAT THE BLOAT*

BY DEBBY HAYES

TABLE OF CONTENTS

INTRODUCTION

As a dietitian, I have talked to more than my fair share of people who struggle with gluten. Most of them are self-diagnosed and they are not sure if gluten really is the problem. Occasionally, I will see someone who has been to a long list of doctors in an attempt to find out what is wrong with them, finally to get a diagnosis of celiac disease.

It can be confusing and overwhelming when you are told that you may no longer eat any food that contains gluten. Even the doctors making the diagnosis are often unaware of the impact those words have on a person's life and the lives of those around them. Consulting with a dietitian or nutritionist who is able to guide you and show you that you can still enjoy your food, is well worth it.

Celiac disease and gluten intolerance share the same set of symptoms. When you eat foods that contain gluten, your body reacts to them and you could display symptoms such as those described further down Foods that contain gluten are wheat, barley and rye, and foods made from them. If you stop eating these foods, your symptoms will subside and you'll feel normal again. Even ingesting the smallest amount of this protein can be a problem for people with celiac disease

To overcome the problem of gluten-induced symptoms, it is important to do your research and surround yourself with resources including easy-to-cook meals such as those in this recipe book. Eating a gluten-free diet will become as natural as eating gluten-containing foods was before. You are changing an ingrained, lifetime habit perpetuated by your upbringing, your peers and the food industry. So, give yourself time to learn how your new diet can work for you.

I often hear that someone has cut out bread and so is eating 'gluten-free'. If only it were that simple. When you remove gluten from your diet, it means cutting out pizza and pasta, avoiding sweet, baked treats and most processed food. It means being aware of what goes into all of your food by reading the food labels as though your life depends on it—it does.

Gluten can be found in anything from bread to salad dressing, to soups and gravies. It is used to improve the texture of food and prevent ingredients from separating; it is one of the most-used ingredients that food manufacturers use, thus making it difficult to avoid completely. But it is not impossible.

Whether you are avoiding gluten because you believe that it is not healthy to consume it— especially in the quantities we do in modern society—or if you have been diagnosed with gluten sensitivity, you will need to know how to make the foods you love, but with different ingredients. You have not been sentenced to a life of boring, tasteless food.

The collection of recipes in this book is here to make your diet interesting again. Say goodbye to bland, boring food. Bring back breads, pasta and pizza; the cakes, cookies and doughnuts; the soups, gravies and creamy sauces. The recipes can be enjoyed by you and your whole family.

WHAT IS GLUTEN?

When you need to follow a gluten-free diet, you should know what it is you are avoiding. A lot of people think it is just a matter of avoiding wheat, but gluten is a naturally occurring protein found in several grains. In fact, gluten is not a single protein but rather the umbrella name for a collection of different proteins or prolamins.

All prolamins have similar structures and are related to each other. They also have similar properties. In wheat, the two most common proteins are gliadin and glutenin; in barley, it is hordein and glutelin; in rye, the proteins are albumin and globulin.

When you have to follow a gluten-free diet, you will be advised to avoid wheat, barley and rye. You may also be told to avoid oats because it is stored, processed and transported using the same equipment that is used for the other grains, which may result in cross-contamination.

Gluten gives bread dough its structure, forming a matrix that traps air and stretches, allowing the dough to rise. Extra gluten is often added to baked goods to increase their strength and improve their texture. The light sponginess of cakes is also due to the effect of gluten.

Manufacturers have found gluten to be such a useful substance that it is added to many different kinds of food that you wouldn't expect to find it in. The reason for the inclusion is it improves the texture and promotes moisture retention in processed food products.

WHY GLUTEN IS BAD FOR SOME PEOPLE

It is estimated that people eating the average western diet consume between five and twenty grams of gluten per day in the form of grains and gluten-containing foods. Most people don't have a problem with gluten, however, the number of people being forced to cut out gluten is rising.

The necessity for gluten-free diets has become quite controversial because gluten is very often blamed for everything that goes wrong in the body. For those people who have a diagnosed gluten sensitivity, though, cutting out this contentious protein brings relief from a variety of symptoms.

Many of the problems associated with gluten arise due to poor gut health and an imbalanced gut microbiome. It might be a bit unpleasant to think about, but we have trillions of bacteria, fungi and viruses living in our digestive systems. In a healthy gut, most of the bacteria are beneficial to our health, but when the balance is disturbed the harmful microbes become more active and cause damage to the body.

The effect of an unhealthy gut microbiome is the incidence of a gluten-induced 'leaky gut'. Normally, the intestinal cell wall strictly controls what passes through it from the intestines to the bloodstream. The structures involved can be weakened when the wrong bacteria are flourishing in the gut resulting in a high intake of gluten. That means that large particles such as undigested proteins and gluten, for example, can pass through the gut wall and enter circulation in the body. From there, they can go anywhere and cause a multitude of seemingly unrelated symptoms.

SIGNS OF A GLUTEN PROBLEM

Not all reactions to wheat are due to the protein, gluten. The immune system can be sensitive to any of the components in the grain, including the other proteins and the carbohydrates. The allergy could be severe and needs a proper diagnosis.

People who need to eliminate gluten from their diets suffer from one of two conditions:

1. Celiac disease
2. Non-celiac gluten sensitivity

CELIAC DISEASE

Celiac disease is the most severe condition related to gluten. If gluten is not removed from the diet entirely, people with celiac disease will continue to suffer from a range of symptoms and the severity of the condition and the complications that arise as a result get progressively worse.

Even though there is a long list of symptoms and complications which arise from celiac disease, many people don't know they have it. Not everyone presents with severe symptoms. It is worth noting though that celiac disease has a genetic component and tends to run in families. If someone in your immediate family is diagnosed with the condition, there is a chance that you are also at risk of developing it.

Celiac disease is an autoimmune condition. The lining of the small intestine of someone with celiac disease comes under attack by their own immune system. It damages structures called villi—finger-like projections that line the small intestine—that create a larger surface area for the absorption of nutrients.

How do you know if you have celiac disease? Symptoms vary from person to person, but these are the most common things to be aware of:

- Abdominal pain
- Cramping
- Bloating
- Gas
- Constipation
- Diarrhea
- Joint pain
- Fatigue
- Malnutrition
- Anemia
- Weight loss
- Skin rashes and itching
- Delayed growth in children

If gluten is not removed from the diet, the long-term complications of celiac disease include the development of more autoimmune disorders, problems with fertility, bowel cancer and neurological conditions.

GLUTEN INTOLERANCE

The official name for gluten intolerance is non-celiac, gluten sensitivity. It affects a lot more people than celiac disease does. But, because there are no definitive tests for it, it is not frequently diagnosed. People who suffer from gluten intolerance have a reaction to gluten in the gut, but it doesn't cause damage to the lining of the intestines as it does in celiac disease.

The symptoms of gluten intolerance are very similar to celiac disease:

- Abdominal pain
- Cramping
- Bloating
- Constipation
- Diarrhea
- Nausea
- Vomiting
- Weight changes
- Joint pain
- Brain fog
- Migraines
- Fatigue
- Skin rashes and itching

The best way to determine if you have gluten intolerance is to remove gluten from your diet for two to four weeks, keeping a record of your symptoms and their severity. If the problem is resolved when you are not eating gluten, there is a good chance that you are intolerant to the protein.

BECOME A FOOD LABEL EXPERT

Gluten is not only found in the most obvious places. It occurs naturally in wheat, barley and rye. If a gluten-free diet was simply about avoiding these grains, it would be fairly easy to do. But, because of the properties it gives to processed foods, it is added to seemingly innocent foods as a binder to hold ingredients together.

When you have a problem with gluten you must become an expert at reading food labels. You cannot rely on food manufacturers to bring your attention to all the ingredients in the product that contains gluten. If wheat, barley or rye are used to make a food product, food labeling laws dictate that they must be disclosed. But it is not mandatory to highlight other ingredients in the product that are made using these grains.

It is therefore essential for you to become familiar with commonly used food ingredients that are made from gluten, or gluten-containing grains. The best thing to do is to make everything yourself, but that is not always practical. Make it a habit to read food labels to identify potentially harmful ingredients before adding any processed food products to your shopping trolley. Even if it is a product you have been using for a long time; manufacturers often change their recipes.

You will have noticed that some products are labeled "Gluten-Free". For the manufacturer to be able to use that label, the food must contain less than a specified amount of gluten, usually less than twenty parts per million. It has been determined that is a safe level for people who have gluten sensitivities. The products that meet these standards have to be submitted for ongoing analysis of all the ingredients used in them as well as the finished product. Not only that but the factories have to be inspected as well to ensure that the equipment is clean and free from gluten.

Foods that contain gluten and those that don't

Foods to avoid: Foods that contain gluten	Foods to include Gluten-free foods
Bread, croissants, bagels, naan, flatbread	Quinoa
Bread crumbs or crumbing mixtures	Rice
Croutons	Buckwheat
Flour tortillas	Sorghum
Breakfast cereals - except those on the gluten-free list	Tapioca
Pasta	Millet
Noodles	Amaranth
Couscous	Teff
Baked foods such as cakes, cookies, muffins, doughnuts etc	Arrowroot
Waffles	Gluten-free oats
Pancakes	Fresh fruit
Crackers	Fresh vegetables
Pastry	Legumes
Soups - fresh, canned and powdered	Nuts
Salad dressing	Seeds
Convenience meals	Red meat
Vegan/vegetarian meat substitutes	Poultry
Stuffing	Fish and seafood
Seasoning mixes	Unflavored soy products such as tofu and tempeh
Sauces and gravies	Dairy products: milk, cheese, yogurt (check the label), butter, cream
Battered or crumbed foods	Cooking oils
Processed meats	Water
Candy and candy bars	Coffee
Brown rice syrup	Tea
Soy sauce	100% fruit juice
Beer	White vinegar
Whiskey	Distilled vinegar
Gin	
Vodka	

Common ingredients that contain gluten

All-purpose flour	Wheat
Semolina	Rye
Durum wheat	Barley
Malt	Spelt
Malted barley	Millet
Malted milk	Einkorn wheat
Malted syrup	KAMUT (Khorasan wheat)
Malt extract	Triticale
Wheatberries	Brewer's yeast
Emmer	Seitan (Vegan meat alternative made from gluten)
Spelt	Wheat starch
Farina	Wheat flour, bread flour
Hydrolyzed wheat protein	Bulgar
Hydrolyzed wheat starch	Modified starch
Hydrolyzed vegetable protein	Natural or artificial flavoring

USEFUL INGREDIENT SUBSTITUTIONS

There is a long list of foods and ingredients to look out for. Navigating the grocery store may seem a bit overwhelming at first. But, as with all new habits, it becomes easier with time.

The first step toward an easy gluten-free diet is to buy naturally gluten-free foods. It might mean you have to make some changes to your old shopping list. As a general rule, unless it is wheat, barley or rye, if you are buying whole, minimally processed food, you can be certain that it won't contain the offending protein. As soon as your food comes with a complicated label and a long list of ingredients your chance of being exposed to gluten rises.

The greatest challenge is to find suitable substitutes for flour. No single flour substitute can match the quality the gluten in wheat flour gives to baked goods. But, that doesn't mean you can no longer enjoy bread, cakes, waffles and doughnuts. You just have to be smart about which flour or flours you use.

To achieve the desired results in taste and texture, two or more gluten-free flours need to be combined. The characteristics of each flour vary:

- **Almond flour:** Made from finely ground almonds, it has a high protein content and a moderate amount of fiber
- **Amaranth flour:** Made from ground amaranth grain, it has a moderate amount of protein and fiber
- **Arrowroot:** Made from arrowroot, a starchy rhizome, it creates a pleasing texture in baked foods and has thickening properties similar to corn starch
- **Brown rice flour:** Made by grinding brown rice, it has a moderate amount of protein and fiber and can create volume in baked foods
- **Coconut flour:** Made from dried coconut that has had the fat removed, it is high in fiber and low in starch and absorbs a lot of liquid
- **Chickpea flour:** Made from chickpeas, it is high in protein and fiber

- **Millet flour:** Made by grinding millet, it has a moderate amount of protein and fiber and produces a fine crumb in baked goods
- **Potato starch:** Made from starchy potatoes and results in a tender, fine crumb in baked foods
- **Sorghum flour:** Made from ground sorghum grain, it has a moderate protein and fiber content
- **Tapioca starch:** Made from the cassava root, it is used for its thickening and gelling properties

While you can mix your own flours to achieve the results your dish requires, there are flour blends available for you to buy. They will contain other ingredients such as xanthan gum and guar gum that will help to enhance the texture of your food. For general baking purposes, it is recommended that you use gluten-free, all-purpose flour. It can be substituted in the same quantities as wheat flour.

MAKING GLUTEN-FREE FAMILY-FRIENDLY

One of the hardest things to do, especially for children, is to watch other people eat the foods they love, knowing that they cannot dig in too. When it is your own family members who are eating the bread and cakes that you long for, it is even more difficult. While you may not want to force your entire family to follow a strictly gluten-free diet, it is much easier for the person doing the shopping and preparing the food if everyone eats the same thing.

This is especially important for people with celiac disease. Even the smallest amount of gluten could trigger their symptoms. If everyone in the house eats gluten-free meals, it helps to reduce the risk of cross-contamination. Dad's toast crumbs that are left at the bottom of the toaster are going to contaminate Mom's carefully selected gluten-free bread.

Using the recipes we have carefully researched and compiled for you, it is possible to make all of your favorite food without running the risk of anyone feeling left out. Whether it is bread for sandwiches, pancakes for breakfast, thick, creamy soup or your aunt's delicious dessert, it is possible to make it gluten-free.

YOU CAN STILL ENJOY YOUR FAVORITE TREATS

The number of people who cannot tolerate gluten due to celiac disease or non-celiac, gluten sensitivity is rising at alarming rates. It may be due to changes in the amount of gluten in our grains or the structure of the gluten, or the amount of gluten we are exposed to in our modern Western diet.

Food labels have to draw your attention to wheat, barley and rye if they are used in the product. But they don't have to highlight other ingredients that may contain gluten. If a food product meets the requirements to be labeled as gluten-free, they can place that claim on the packaging. To maintain that claim, the food and the factory must be inspected and tested regularly.

There is a long list of foods you need to avoid, but it cannot be denied that the list of foods you CAN eat is even longer. You may have to put a little extra thought into your meals, but by using fresh, unprocessed ingredients, and a range of different flours, you have the potential to create lip-smackingly delicious meals that can be enjoyed by the whole family.

Rather than focusing on the negative, turn your attention to the new possibilities in food recipes you can explore. Harness your cooking creativity and dig into new flavors, and familiar ones made from different ingredients. These recipes were compiled with you in mind. We want to challenge you to try something new, but we also want to show you how to make your old favorites but use foods that don't make you feel sick.

BREAKFASTS

BANANA CUPS

PREP TIME: 5 MIN | SERVES: 4

INGREDIENTS:

- 1 cup raw walnuts
- 2 ripe bananas
- ½ cup brewed coffee
- ¼ cup coconut oil, melted
- 1 tsp chocolate or vanilla extract
- Pinch fine salt

DIRECTIONS:

1. In a blender, add the walnuts, bananas, coffee, coconut oil, chocolate or vanilla extract and fine salt. Purée until smooth.

2. Divide the banana mixture into 4 small bowls.

3. Enjoy immediately.

Recipe Tip: for a firm banana filling, cover the bowls with plastic wrap and refrigerate overnight.

CRANBERRY GRANOLA

COOK TIME: 25 MIN | MAKES: 8 CUPS

INGREDIENTS:

- 6 cups gluten-free oats
- 1 cup pecan nuts, roughly chopped
- ¼ cup sunflower oil
- ¼ cup organic honey
- 1 tsp vanilla extract
- 2 tsp ground cinnamon
- ⅛ tsp fine salt
- 1 cup dried cranberries

DIRECTIONS:

1. Heat the oven to 325°F or 170°C.

2. In a large mixing bowl, add the gluten-free oats and pecan nuts, mix to combine.

3. In a large measuring jug, add the sunflower oil, organic honey, vanilla extract, ground cinnamon and fine salt, and whisk to combine.

4. Pour the liquid mixture over the oats and pecans, mix to coat.

5. Spread the coated mixture onto a non-stick baking sheet.

6. Bake for 15 minutes. Use a spatula to mix the granola halfway through baking. Bake for 5 minutes more and mix again.

7. Bake for a further 5 minutes until the mixture is golden brown.

8. Allow the mixture to cool completely before mixing in the dried cranberries.

9. Store in an airtight container.

STRAWBERRY MUFFINS

COOK TIME: 18 MIN | MAKES: 18

INGREDIENTS:

- Non-stick cooking spray
- 2 cups almond flour
- 2 tbsp granulated sugar
- 1 tsp baking powder
- ½ tsp baking soda
- ¼ tsp fine salt
- ½ cup almond milk, room temperature
- ½ cup organic honey
- ⅓ cup sunflower oil
- 2 large eggs, room temperature
- 1 tbsp apple cider vinegar
- 1 tbsp almond butter
- 1 tsp vanilla extract
- ⅔ cup strawberries, chopped

DIRECTIONS:

1. Preheat the oven to 350°F or 180°C. Coat a cupcake baking pan with non-stick cooking spray, and set aside.

2. In the bowl of a stand mixer, add the almond flour, granulated sugar, baking powder, baking soda, and fine salt, and mix to combine.

3. In a large measuring jug, add the almond milk, organic honey, sunflower oil, eggs, apple cider vinegar, almond butter, and vanilla extract, and whisk to combine.

4. Make a well in the center of the dry ingredients and slowly pour in the wet ingredients. Mix on low speed until fully incorporated.

5. Allow the batter to rest for 5 minutes until slightly thickened, fold in the chopped strawberries.

6. Fill each cupcake cup three-quarters full of batter. Bake for 13 to 18 minutes, or until the edges are golden brown and a toothpick inserted comes out clean.

7. Allow to cool for 5 minutes before removing from the tin.

8. Transfer the cupcakes onto a wire rack and cool completely before serving.

PINEAPPLE BANANA LOAF

COOK TIME: 25 MIN | MAKES: 1 LOAF

INGREDIENTS:

- Non-stick cooking spray
- 1 cup granulated sugar
- 2 ½ ripe bananas, mashed
- ½ can (10 oz) crushed pineapple, drained
- ⅔ cup brown rice flour
- 1 cup almond flour
- ⅔ cup tapioca flour
- ⅓ cup water
- ⅓ cup unsalted butter, melted
- 2 large eggs
- 1 tsp baking soda
- ½ tsp fine salt
- ¼ tsp baking powder

DIRECTIONS:

1. Preheat the oven to 350°F or 180°C. Coat a 5-by-9-inch loaf pan with non-stick cooking spray.

2. In a large-sized mixing bowl, add the sugar, mashed bananas, crushed pineapple, brown rice flour, almond flour, tapioca flour, water, melted butter, eggs, baking soda, fine salt, and baking powder, and whisk until fully incorporated.

3. Allow the batter to stand for 5 minutes, and then pour the batter into the coated loaf pan.

4. Bake for 20 to 25 minutes until golden and a toothpick inserted comes out clean.

5. Allow to cool for 5 to 10 minutes in the pan before placing it on a wire rack to cool completely. Slice and serve.

ALMOND RAISIN FLAPJACK

COOK TIME: 5 MIN | SERVES: 6

INGREDIENTS:

- 1 cup almond flour
- ¾ cup buckwheat flour
- 2 tsp baking powder
- 1 tsp fine salt
- ½ tsp ground cinnamon
- 1¾ cups almond milk
- 3 large eggs, separated
- 4 tbsp unsalted butter, melted and cooled
- 2 tbsp maple syrup
- 1–2 tsp sunflower oil
- ½ cup raisins

DIRECTIONS:

1. In a medium-sized mixing bowl, add the almond flour, buckwheat flour, baking powder, fine salt, and ground cinnamon, and whisk to combine. In a separate mixing bowl, add the almond milk, egg yolks, melted butter, and maple syrup, and whisk to combine.

2. Using a hand mixer, beat the egg whites on high speed for 3 to 4 minutes until stiff peaks form.

3. Pour the milk mixture into the flour mixture and whisk for 1 minute until the batter has thickened, and no lumps remain.

4. Gently fold in the stiff egg whites until just combined.

5. Heat 1 tsp of sunflower oil in a nonstick skillet or crêpe pan over medium heat for 3 to 5 minutes until shimmering.

6. Use a 1 oz ladle of batter per flapjack and sprinkle 1 tbsp of raisins over each flapjack.

7. Cook for 2 to 3 minutes until the bottoms of the flapjacks are brown and the surface starts to bubble.

8. Flip flapjacks and cook for 1 to 2 minutes longer until browned. Use the remaining 1 tsp of sunflower oil as needed and repeat with the remaining batter and raisins.

9. Serve immediately.

LIME FETA FLAPJACKS

COOK TIME: 5 MIN | SERVES: 4

INGREDIENTS:

- ⅔ cup Bob's Red Mill gluten-free 1-to-1 baking flour
- ½ tsp baking soda
- ½ cup feta cheese, crumbled
- 2 large eggs, separated
- ⅓ cup almond milk
- 1 tsp grated lime zest
- 4 tsp lime juice
- ½ tsp vanilla extract
- 2 tsp unsalted butter, melted and cooled
- Pinch cream of tartar
- ¼ cup granulated sugar
- 1–2 tsp sunflower oil

DIRECTIONS:

1. In a medium-sized mixing bowl, add the gluten-free flour and baking soda, and mix to combine. Make a well in the center of the flour and add the crumbled feta, egg yolks, almond milk, lime zest, lime juice vanilla extract, and whisk to combine. Mix in the melted butter.

2. Using a hand mixer, beat the egg whites and the cream of tartar on medium speed until soft peaks form.

3. Gradually add the sugar and beat for 1 to 2 minutes until glossy and stiff peaks form.

4. Place about a 1/3 of the whipped egg whites into the batter and whisk gently until the mixture has lightened.

5. Use a silicone spatula to gently fold in the remaining egg whites into the batter.

6. Heat 1 teaspoon of sunflower oil in a nonstick skillet or crêpe pan over medium heat for 3 to 5 minutes until shimmering.

7. Use a 1 oz ladle or 1/4 cup to portion the batter, leaving 2 inches between each portion.

8. Cook for 2½ minutes until the bottoms of the flapjacks are brown and the surface starts to bubble.

9. Flip the flapjacks and continue to cook for 2½ minutes until the other side is golden brown. Repeat with the remaining sunflower oil and batter.

10. Serve immediately.

Tip: serve these flapjacks with your choice of gluten-free topping or pie filling.

CHOCONUT GRANOLA

PREP TIME: 5 MIN | SERVES: 1

INGREDIENTS:

- ½ cup vanilla cashew milk
- 2 tbsp organic cashew butter
- ½ tbsp 100% cocoa powder
- 1 ripe banana, peeled and mashed
- 1 tbsp honey
- ½ cup blueberry granola

DIRECTIONS:

1. In a small airtight container with a lid, add the cashew milk, cashew butter, cocoa powder, mashed banana, and honey, and mix to combine.

2. Add the granola and mix. Press the granola down with a spoon making sure that it is covered by the milk.

3. Place the lid on top and refrigerate overnight.

HONEY HAM POTATOES

COOK TIME: 35 MIN | SERVES: 4

INGREDIENTS:

- 3 cups russet potatoes, peeled and diced
- 4 tbsp sunflower oil
- 1 red onion, peeled and chopped
- 1 tsp fine salt
- ½ tsp ground black pepper
- 2 cups honey ham, diced

DIRECTIONS:

1. Fill a large stockpot with water and add ½ tsp of fine salt, and bring to a boil over high heat.

2. Add the diced potatoes and cook for 15 minutes until tender. Drain and set aside.

3. In a large, nonstick frying pan, heat the sunflower oil over medium-high heat until hot.

4. Add the chopped onions, ½ tsp fine salt, and ground black pepper, and mix to combine.

5. Fry for 5 minutes until the onions have softened.

6. Mix in the diced honey ham and cook for 3 minutes until lightly browned.

7. Add the drained potatoes and cook for 6 minutes.

8. Gently press the hash down, flip with a spatula, and cook for a further 6 minutes until the potatoes are browned and the ham is crisp. Serve warm.

SAVORY MUFFINS

COOK TIME: 15 MIN | SERVES: 6

INGREDIENTS:

- Non-stick cooking spray
- 12 large eggs
- ¼ tsp fine salt
- 1½ cups kale, finely chopped
- ½ cup sun-dried tomatoes, chopped
- ½ cup red onion, chopped
- ½ cup feta cheese, crumbled

DIRECTIONS:

1. Preheat the oven to 350°F or 180°C. Coat a 12-cup muffin tin with non-stick cooking spray.

2. In a large-sized mixing bowl, add the eggs and fine salt, and whisk until foamy.

3. Divide the chopped kale, chopped tomatoes, and chopped onion among the 12 muffin cups and sprinkle each cup with crumbled feta cheese.

4. Using a ladle, pour the egg mixture evenly among the 12 muffin cups. Bake for 15 minutes or until set.

5. Allow to cool for 5 minutes before serving.

Ingredient Tip: add 1 tbsp of chopped parsley or basil to the whisked egg for extra flavor.

SWEET POTATO FRY

COOK TIME: 20 MIN | SERVES: 4

INGREDIENTS:

- 2 tbsp sunflower oil, divided
- 2 sweet potatoes, peeled and diced
- 1 small courgette, diced
- 1 green bell pepper, seeded and thinly sliced
- ½ red onion, thinly sliced
- Fine salt
- Ground black pepper
- 1 tbsp arugula, roughly chopped
- 1 tbsp basil, roughly chopped
- 4 eggs

DIRECTIONS:

1. Heat 1 tablespoon of sunflower oil in a large heavy bottom pan over medium-high heat until hot.

2. Add the diced sweet potatoes and cook for 5 minutes.

3. Add the diced courgette and fry for 2 to 3 minutes.

4. Push the vegetables to the side of the pan and add the sliced green pepper and sliced onion, fry for 2 to 3 minutes.

5. Combine all and season with fine salt and ground black pepper to taste.

6. Continue cooking for 5 minutes until the sweet potatoes are soft.

7. Transfer the vegetables onto a serving dish and sprinkle with chopped arugula and chopped basil.

8. Add the remaining tablespoon of sunflower oil to the pan and cook the eggs to your liking. Serve the eggs over the vegetable hash.

Recipe Tip: omit the eggs for an allergy-free dish.

OVEN EGG TOAST

COOK TIME: 45 MIN | SERVES: 8

INGREDIENTS:

- Non-stick cooking spray
- 1 loaf gluten-free bread, cubed
- ⅓ cup cashew nuts, chopped
- 7 large eggs
- 2 cups cashew milk
- ¼ cup organic honey
- 1 ½ tbsp vanilla extract
- 2 ½ tsp ground cinnamon, divided
- ½ tsp ground allspice
- 5 tbsp cold unsalted butter, sliced
- ½ cup light brown sugar
- ½ cup honey, for serving

DIRECTIONS:

1. Coat a 9-by-13-inch baking dish with non-stick cooking spray.

2. Place the cubed bread at the bottom of the baking dish and sprinkle with chopped cashew nuts.

3. In a medium-sized mixing bowl, add the eggs, cashew milk, organic honey, vanilla extract, 1½ teaspoons of ground cinnamon, and ground allspice. Mix well.

4. Carefully pour the egg mixture over the bread and mix to coat. Cover with aluminum foil and refrigerate overnight.

5. Preheat the oven to 375°F or 190°C and remove the bread mixture from the refrigerator.

6. In a small-sized mixing bowl, add the remaining 1 teaspoon of ground cinnamon, cold butter slices, and brown sugar. Combine the ingredients until crumbly. Sprinkle the mixture on top of the bread and replace the foil.

7. Bake, covered, for 25 minutes, then uncover and bake for a further 20 minutes until golden brown and hot.

8. Allow to cool for 5 minutes before cutting. Drizzle with honey and serve warm.

Substitution Tip: replace the honey with powdered sugar or maple syrup.

LEMON BLUEBERRY MUFFINS

COOK TIME: 20 MIN | MAKES: 12

INGREDIENTS:

- 2 cups blueberries
- ¾ cup granulated sugar
- ½ cup raw walnuts
- 2 tsp grated lemon zest
- 2 cups Bob's Red Mill gluten-free 1-to-1 baking flour
- 1 tbsp baking powder
- ½ tsp salt
- ¼ tsp xanthan gum
- 8 tbsp unsalted butter, melted and cooled
- ½ cup plain yogurt
- 3 large eggs
- Non-stick cooking spray
- 2 tbsp light brown sugar

DIRECTIONS:

1. In a food processor, pulse the blueberries 4 to 5 times until coarsely chopped. Transfer to a bowl and set aside.

2. Using the same food processor, add the granulated sugar, walnuts, and lemon zest and process for 10 to 15 seconds until it resembles coarse sand.

3. Add the gluten-free flour, baking powder, salt, and xanthan gum and pulse 5 to 10 times until combined.

4. In a large-sized bowl with a lid, add the melted butter, plain yogurt, and eggs, and whisk until well combined.

5. Add the wet ingredients to the food processor and process for 30 seconds until well combined and no lumps remain.

6. Using a silicone spatula, scrape the batter into the now-empty bowl and fold in the chopped blueberries; the batter should be thick and stiff. Cover the bowl with the lid and allow the batter to rest for 30 minutes at room temperature.

7. Preheat the oven to 400°F or 200°C. Coat a muffin pan with non-stick cooking spray.

8. Use an ice cream scoop to portion the batter into the prepared muffin pan. Sprinkle the light brown sugar over the top of the batter.

9. Bake for 16 to 20 minutes, rotating the pan halfway until muffins are golden, and a toothpick inserted comes out clean.

10. Allow the muffins to cool in the pan on a wire rack for 10 minutes. Transfer the muffins from the pan to the wire rack and let them cool for another 10 minutes before serving.

PECAN NUT LOAF

COOK TIME: 1 HOUR | MAKES: 1 LOAF

INGREDIENTS:

- Non-stick cooking spray
- 2 cups Bob's Red Mill gluten-free 1-to-1 baking flour
- 1 ½ tsp baking soda
- 1 tsp baking powder
- ½ tsp salt
- ¼ tsp xanthan gum
- ¾ cup dark brown sugar
- 1 cup buttermilk
- 6 tbsp butter, melted
- 2 large eggs
- 1 cup pitted dates, chopped
- 1 cup pecan nuts, chopped

DIRECTIONS:

1. Preheat the oven to 350°F or 180°C. Coat an 8½ by 4½-inch loaf pan with non-stick cooking spray.

2. In a large-sized mixing bowl, add the flour, baking soda, baking powder, salt, and xanthan gum, and whisk to combine.

3. In a separate mixing bowl, add the brown sugar, buttermilk, melted butter and eggs, and whisk to combine.

4. Use a whisk to gently fold the buttermilk mixture into the flour mixture for 1 minute until combined and no lumps remain. Fold in the chopped dates and chopped pecan nuts.

5. Scrape the batter into the prepared loaf pan and smooth the top.

6. Bake for 1 hour rotating the pan halfway until it is a deep golden brown and a toothpick inserted comes out clean.

7. Allow the bread to cool in the pan for 20 minutes, then remove and let it cool on a wire rack for 1 hour before serving.

Substitution Tip: use 1 cup of unsweetened soy milk mixed with 1 tablespoon white vinegar or lemon juice for dairy-free buttermilk.

BACON TATER BAKE

COOK TIME: 45 MIN | SERVES: 12

INGREDIENTS:

- Non-stick cooking spray
- 1 lb. gluten-free bacon, chopped
- 12 oz package gluten-free maple syrup breakfast sausage
- 1 (32 oz) package Tater Tots, gluten free
- 12 large eggs
- ½ cup milk
- ½ red onion, finely chopped
- ½ tbsp garlic, crushed
- ½ tsp fine salt
- ¼ tsp ground black pepper

DIRECTIONS:

1. Preheat the oven to 350°F or 180°C.

2. Coat a deep baking pan with non-stick cooking spray.

3. In a heavy bottom frying pan over medium-high heat, fry the bacon for 3 minutes until brown and crispy. Place the bacon on paper towels and allow to cool for 5 minutes. Discard the bacon grease.

4. In the same pan, fry the breakfast sausage for 5 minutes on each side until cooked through. Transfer to the plate with the bacon. Allow to cool for 1 minute and cut into pieces.

5. Place the Tater Tots in a single layer in the prepared baking dish.

6. In a medium-sized mixing bowl, add the eggs, milk, chopped onion, crushed garlic, fine salt, and ground black pepper, and whisk to combine. Mix in the fried bacon and sausage. Pour the mixture over the Tater Tots.

7. Bake for 40–45 minutes until the egg mixture is set. Allow it to stand for 10 minutes before serving.

Tip: add chopped parsley or Italian herbs to the dish for extra flavor.

Recipe tip: Tater Tots is mashed potatoes that are shaped into a ball or log, deep fried or baked.

TOMATO POACHED EGGS

COOK TIME: 15 MIN | SERVES: 6

INGREDIENTS:

- 3 tbsp canola oil
- 1–2 shallots, peeled and chopped
- 2 green bell peppers, seeded and chopped
- 1 tbsp garlic, minced
- 1 tsp ground coriander
- 1 tsp smoked paprika
- ½ tsp ground cumin
- 1 tsp molasses (optional)
- 1 (28 oz) can whole peeled tomatoes, with the juices
- ½ tsp fine salt
- ¼ tsp ground black pepper
- 1 tsp granulated sugar
- 6 large eggs
- ¼ cup fresh coriander, finely chopped

DIRECTIONS:

1. Heat the canola oil in a large heavy bottom pan over medium heat until hot. Add the chopped shallots and chopped green bell peppers, and fry for 5 minutes, mixing occasionally until the onions become translucent.

2. Add the minced garlic, ground coriander, smoked paprika, ground cumin and molasses (if using), and cook for 1 minute, stirring until fragrant.

3. Add the canned tomatoes with their juice, breaking the tomatoes down with a fork. Add fine salt, ground black pepper, and granulated sugar, mix to incorporate, and allow the mixture to simmer.

4. Use a spoon to make six small wells in the sauce and crack an egg into each well.

5. Cover the pan with a lid and cook for 5–8 minutes or until the eggs are poached to your liking.

6. Spoon an egg and sauce onto each plate and serve warm. Garnish with chopped coriander.

SNACKS & APPETIZERS

DRIED FRUIT BARS

COOK TIME: 25 MIN | MAKES: 8 BARS

INGREDIENTS:

- 3 tbsp sunflower oil, divided
- 2 cups gluten-free rolled oats
- ½ cup sunflower seeds, toasted
- ½ cup sliced almonds
- 1 cup dried berries & golden raisins mix
- ¼ cup flax meal
- 1 tsp ground cinnamon
- ¾ cup maple syrup
- ½ tsp fine salt
- 1 teaspoon vanilla extract

DIRECTIONS:

1. Preheat the oven to 325°F or 170°C.

2. Coat the inside of a baking sheet with 1 tablespoon of sunflower oil.

3. In a large-sized mixing bowl, add the rolled oats, toasted sunflower seeds, sliced almonds, dried berries & golden raisins mix, flax meal and ground cinnamon, and mix to combine.

4. In a microwave-safe jug, add the maple syrup, the remaining 2 tablespoons sunflower oil, fine salt and vanilla extract, and whisk to combine.

5. Heat the liquid mixture in the microwave for 1½ minutes, pour over the oat mixture, and mix to coat.

6. Spread the oat mixture over the prepared baking sheet, pressing down with your fingers and palms until tightly packed.

7. Bake for 20 to 25 minutes until lightly browned. Cool and cut into bars.

GUACAMOLE RICE ROLLS

COOK TIME: 5 MIN | MAKES: 8 ROLLS

INGREDIENTS:

Dipping Sauce:
- 4 tsp apple cider vinegar
- 1 tsp balsamic vinegar
- ½ cup honey
- ½ cup pine nuts
- ½ cup parsley, roughly chopped
- 1 garlic clove, minced
- 4 spring onions, sliced
- 1 tbsp granulated sugar
- 1 tsp ground coriander
- ¼ cup sunflower oil

Filling:
- 1 red onion, finely chopped
- 2 ripe avocados, peeled, pitted, and mashed
- 1 tomato, seeds removed and diced
- ¼ tsp parsley, finely chopped
- ¼ tsp smoked paprika
- Fine salt
- Freshly ground black pepper

For the guacamole rice rolls:
- 8 (8") round rice paper wrappers
- 2 cups sunflower oil

DIRECTIONS:

For the Sauce:

1. In a medium-sized microwave-safe bowl, add the apple cider vinegar, balsamic vinegar and honey, microwave for 1 minute, then mix.
2. In a food processor, add the pine nuts, chopped parsley, minced garlic, sliced spring onions, granulated sugar and ground coriander, and purée until smooth.
3. Add the pine nut mixture and sunflower oil into the vinegar mixture and whisk to combine. Refrigerate.

For the filling:

1. In a medium-sized mixing bowl, add the chopped red onion, mashed avocado, diced tomato, chopped parsley, and smoked paprika. Mix to combine. Season with salt and pepper.

For the guacamole rice rolls:

1. Soften the rice paper in warm water for 3 seconds. Place the rice papers on a clean surface, smooth side down.
2. Spoon 2 tablespoons of the guacamole filling in the center of the rice paper. Fold the left and right edges inward, then starting from the bottom, roll up to cover the filling. Keep rolling until you reach the end. Place on a plate and repeat with remaining rice paper wrappers.
3. Heat the sunflower oil in a large heavy bottom pan over medium heat.
4. Fry the rice rolls in batches for 2 minutes on each side until lightly golden.
5. Remove with a slotted spoon and drain on a paper towel-lined plate.
6. Serve with dipping sauce.

HAM PIZZA CUPS

COOK TIME: 15 MIN | MAKES: 12

INGREDIENTS:

- Non-stick cooking spray
- 2 large eggs, beaten
- ½ tsp garlic powder
- 1 tsp finely chopped basil
- 1 tsp dried oregano
- 1 ⅓ cups Gluten-free Pancake & Waffle Mix
- ½ cup water
- ⅓ cup vegetable oil
- 1 ½ cups gluten-free shredded Colby Monterey Jack cheese, divided
- 1 ½ cups gluten-free ham, chopped
- ¾ cup gluten-free tomato basil sauce

DIRECTIONS:

1. Preheat the oven to 425°F or 220°C. Coat a muffin tin with non-stick cooking spray.

2. In a medium-sized mixing bowl, add the beaten eggs, garlic powder, chopped basil, and dried oregano, and mix until fully combined. Add the gluten-free pancake mix, water, and vegetable oil, and mix to combine again.

3. Fill each muffin cup three-quarters full. Sprinkle 1 tablespoon of shredded cheese and 1 tablespoon of chopped ham over the top of the batter.

4. Spoon 1 tablespoon of tomato basil sauce over the ham and cheese.

5. Add another layer of ham and cheese over the sauce. Bake for 15 minutes. Allow to cool for 2 minutes before removing from pan.

HONEY CASHEW BITES

PREP TIME: 5 MIN | MAKES: 12

INGREDIENTS:

- ½ cup canola oil
- ½ cup creamy cashew butter
- ¼ cup organic honey
- ½ cup 100% cocoa powder
- ½ tsp fine salt

DIRECTIONS:

1. Line a 12-cup muffin pan with paper muffin cups.

2. In a food processor, add the canola oil, cashew butter, organic honey, cocoa powder, and fine salt. Purée until smooth.

3. Divide about 2 to 3 tablespoons of the mixture into each lined muffin cup and refrigerate for 20 minutes. Keep refrigerated.

PEAR FRITTERS

COOK TIME: 14 MIN | MAKES: 8

INGREDIENTS:

- ½ cup chickpea flour
- ½ cup plus 2 tbsp powdered sugar, divided
- 2 tsp baking powder
- 2 tsp ground cinnamon
- ½ tsp ground allspice
- ¼ tsp fine salt
- 3 pears, peeled, cored, and diced
- ½ cup plus 2 tbsp soy milk, divided
- 48 fl. oz canola oil, for frying

DIRECTIONS:

1. In a medium-sized mixing bowl, sift the chickpea flour, ½ cup of powdered sugar, baking powder, ground cinnamon, ground allspice, and fine salt. Mix in the diced pears. Stir in ½ cup of soy milk until no lumps remain.

2. Add the canola oil into a large heavy bottom pan over medium-high heat until hot. Make sure to not leave the oil unattended.

3. Scoop ½ cup of the fritter batter into the hot oil to make one fritter. Repeat with the remaining batter in batches.

4. Cook for 3 minutes, then place a lid on the pan to continue cooking for 2 to 3 minutes more until the top is set.

5. Transfer the cooked fritters onto a wire rack and allow the oil to heat up again before using the remaining batter.

6. In a small-sized mixing bowl, combine the remaining 2 tablespoons powdered sugar with the remaining 2 tablespoons of soy milk.

7. Drizzle the glaze over the cooked fritters. Serve warm.

GARLIC POTATO SPEARS

COOK TIME: 40 MIN | SERVES: 4

INGREDIENTS:

- 2 sweet potatoes, cut into spears
- 3 tsp avocado oil
- ¼ tsp garlic powder
- ¼ tsp garlic, minced

DIRECTIONS:

1. Preheat the oven to 400°F or 200°C.

2. Place the sweet potato spears on a baking sheet. Drizzle the avocado oil over the spears and use a basting brush to coat them fully.

3. Season the spears with garlic powder and minced garlic, making sure they are well coated.

4. Bake for 40 minutes, flipping halfway.

5. For crisper spears, turn the oven to broil and cook for a few extra minutes.

Tip: swap the sweet potatoes for russet potatoes and shorten the bake time by 2 to 3 minutes.

BATTERED ONIONS

COOK TIME: 15 MIN | SERVES: 4

INGREDIENTS:

- 48 fl. oz sunflower oil
- 1 ½ cups Bob's Red Mill gluten-free 1-to-1 baking flour
- 2 tsp Italian seasoning
- 2 tsp freshly ground black pepper
- 2 tsp smoked paprika
- 1 tsp onion powder
- Fine salt
- 1 large egg, beaten
- 1 cup buttermilk
- 3 tbsp organic honey
- 3 tbsp gluten-free sweet chili sauce
- 2 yellow onions, cut into rings

DIRECTIONS:

1. Pour the sunflower oil into a large stockpot and set it over medium heat.

2. In a large mixing bowl, add the gluten-free flour, Italian seasoning, ground black pepper, smoked paprika, onion powder, and fine salt to taste, and mix to combine.

3. In another large mixing bowl, add the beaten egg, buttermilk, organic honey and sweet chili sauce, and mix to combine.

4. To test the oil, drop a small bit of batter into it. If the batter sizzles immediately, the oil is hot enough.

5. Coat each onion ring in the egg mixture, allow the excess to drip off, then dredge it in the flour mixture, making sure the entire onion ring is coated.

6. Working in batches, place each ring in the hot oil and fry for 1 to 3 minutes until golden brown.

7. Once golden, flip and fry the other side for an additional 1 to 3 minutes.

8. Use a slotted spoon to carefully remove the onion rings from the stockpot and place them on a baking sheet lined with paper towels. Repeat with the remaining onion rings.

9. Allow to cool before serving.

Tip: another way to test to see if the oil is hot enough, dip the handle of a wooden spoon in the oil, if you see it sizzling, then the oil is ready.

POLENTA CORNMEAL STICKS

COOK TIME: 15 MIN | SERVES: 4

INGREDIENTS:

- Non-stick cooking spray
- 4 cups water
- 1 tsp fine salt plus extra for seasoning
- Ground black pepper
- 1 cup gluten-free polenta cornmeal mix
- 2 tsp cilantro, finely chopped
- 1 tsp grated lime zest
- ½ cup canola oil

DIRECTIONS:

1. Coat a baking pan with non-stick cooking spray and set aside.

2. In a large-sized stockpot, bring the water to a boil and add the fine salt.

3. Add the polenta mix in a slow stream, stirring constantly with a wooden spoon.

4. Reduce the heat to low and cook for 3 to 5 minutes, uncovered, stirring often until the polenta is soft and smooth.

5. Remove from the heat, add the chopped cilantro and lime zest and season with fine salt and ground black pepper to taste, and combine.

6. Transfer the cooked polenta onto the prepared baking pan. Refrigerate, uncovered for 1 hour until firm and sliceable.

7. Gently place the chilled polenta onto a cutting board, and discard the parchment.

8. Slice the polenta in half lengthwise, then slice each half crosswise into sixteen wide fries. You should have 32 fries in total.

9. Heat the canola oil in a deep nonstick frying pan until hot.

10. Working in batches, fry half of the polenta for 6 to 7 minutes per side until crisp and beginning to brown.

11. Transfer onto a paper towel-lined plate. Repeat with the remaining polenta sticks and serve warm.

Tip: cook the polenta mix the day before and keep refrigerated overnight.

TURKEY BACON SHRIMP

COOK TIME: 15 MIN | SERVES: 5

INGREDIENTS:

- Sealable plastic bag
- ¼ cup light brown sugar
- 1 tsp onion powder
- 1 tbsp garlic powder
- ½ tsp red chili flakes
- ½ tsp cayenne pepper
- ¼ tsp fine salt
- 2 tbsp lemon juice
- 2 tbsp sunflower oil
- 20 large shrimp, peeled and deveined
- Non-stick cooking spray
- 20 strips gluten-free turkey bacon

DIRECTIONS:

1. In a large, sealable plastic bag add the light brown sugar, onion powder, garlic powder, red chili flakes, cayenne pepper, fine salt, lemon juice and sunflower oil, seal the bag and shake to mix.

2. Add the clean shrimp, close the bag, and mix until all the shrimp is covered in the marinade. Refrigerator for 30 minutes.

3. Preheat the oven to 450°F or 230°C. Line a baking pan with aluminum foil and coat with non-stick cooking spray.

4. Wrap each marinaded shrimp with a slice of turkey bacon, and secure with a toothpick.

5. Bake for 10–15 minutes until the turkey bacon is crisp and the shrimp turns pink.

TOMATO, BASIL CROSTINI

COOK TIME: 2 MIN | SERVES: 4

INGREDIENTS:

- 6 large Roma tomatoes, diced
- 6 fresh basil leaves, roughly chopped
- ¼ tsp fine salt
- ¼ tsp ground black pepper
- 1 tbsp garlic, crushed
- 4 tbsp olive oil, divided
- 1 tsp balsamic vinegar
- 1 gluten-free loaf of ciabatta or French bread

DIRECTIONS:

1. In a medium-sized mixing bowl, add the diced tomatoes, chopped basil, fine salt, ground black pepper, crushed garlic, 1 tablespoon olive oil and balsamic vinegar, and mix to combine. Refrigerate for 30 minutes.

2. Preheat the oven to broil. Slice the ciabatta or French bread, and brush with the remaining olive oil. Place the coated bread slices on a non-stick baking pan and broil for 1–2 minutes, or until the bread is toasted.

3. Top with the basil and tomato mixture and serve.

APRICOT SLICES

COOK TIME: 20 MIN | MAKES: 9 SLICES

INGREDIENTS:

- Non-stick cooking spray
- ¼ cup coconut flour
- 1 cup finely ground almond flour
- ¼ cup tapioca flour (starch)
- ½ tsp salt
- ¼ cup coconut oil, melted
- 1 large egg, beaten
- 1 tbsp honey
- 1 ½ cups dried apricots
- ¼ cup light brown sugar
- 1 tbsp lime juice
- ¼ tsp ground allspice

DIRECTIONS:

1. Preheat the oven to 350°F or 180°C. Coat a baking pan with non-stick cooking spray.

2. Blend the coconut flour, almond flour, tapioca flour and fine salt in a food processor, and pulse to combine.

3. Add the melted coconut oil, beaten egg, and honey and pulse until blended.

4. Divide the crust mixture and place half of it onto the prepared baking pan and press it down with your fingertips. Keeping the other half for the topping.

5. In the food processor, add the dried apricots, light brown sugar, lime juice, and ground allspice, and blend until mostly smooth. Spread the apricot mixture over the crust layer.

6. Sprinkle the remaining crust pieces over the top of the apricot mixture. Bake for 20 minutes until the top is lightly browned.

BREADS & CRACKERS

WHITE BREAD

COOK TIME: 45 MIN | MAKES: 1 LOAF

INGREDIENTS:

- Non-stick cooking spray
- ¾ cup water
- 1 pkt fast rising instant yeast
- 3 large egg whites
- ¼ cup canola oil
- 1 ½ tbsp apple cider vinegar
- 3 cups Bob's Red Mill gluten-free 1-to-1 baking flour
- ¼ cup light brown sugar
- 2 ¼ tsp xanthan gum
- ½ tsp baking powder

DIRECTIONS:

1. Coat a loaf pan generously with non-stick cooking spray.

2. In a medium-sized microwave-safe bowl, heat the water for 30 to 45 seconds. Sprinkle the yeast over the warm water and allow it to sit until foamy.

3. Using a stand mixer fitted with a whisk attachment, add the egg whites, and whisk for 5 to 7 minutes, on high speed until stiff peaks form.

4. Reduce the speed to low, add the canola oil, apple cider vinegar, the yeast water, and continue to mix.

5. Add the gluten-free flour, light brown sugar, xanthan gum, and baking powder and continue mixing for 1 to 3 minutes until a smooth dough forms.

6. Transfer the dough into the prepared loaf pan. Cover with a damp clean kitchen towel and allow the dough to rise in a warm place for 1 hour, or until doubled in size.

7. During the last 10 minutes of proofing, preheat the oven to 350°F or 180°C.

8. Bake for 45 minutes until the edges and the top of the bread are golden brown.

9. Cool for 2 to 3 minutes in the pan before transferring to a wire rack to cool completely. Slice and serve.

Tip: to test if the bread is fully cooked, tap the top of the bread with your fingers, if it sounds hollow then it is cooked.

DINNER ROLLS

COOK TIME: 15 MIN | MAKES: 9 ROLLS

INGREDIENTS:

- Non-stick cooking spray
- 1 ¾ cups Bob's Red Mill gluten-free 1-to-1 baking flour
- ½ tsp fine salt
- ½ tsp xanthan gum
- 1 pk fast rising instant yeast
- ½ cup plus 2 tbsp whole milk
- 2 tbsp unsalted butter, softened, plus 2 tbsp melted butter for brushing
- 1 large egg, room temperature
- ¼ cup organic honey
- ½ tsp apple cider vinegar

DIRECTIONS:

1. Using a stand mixer fitted with a dough hook, add the gluten-free flour, fine salt, xanthan gum, and mix to combine.

2. Make a well in the middle of the flour mixture and add the instant yeast.

3. Warm the milk for 45 seconds in the microwave and add the warm milk over the yeast. Allow it to stand for a few minutes until foamy.

4. Add the 2 tablespoons of softened butter, egg, organic honey, and apple cider vinegar, and mix for 2 minutes until fully combined.

5. Coat a deep baking dish and an ice cream scoop with non-stick cooking spray. Scoop equal-size balls of dough into the dish.

6. Cover the pan with a clean, damp kitchen towel and allow the rolls to rise in a warm place for 1 hour, or until doubled in size.

7. During the last 10 minutes of proofing, preheat the oven to 400°F or 200°C and bake for 11 to 13 minutes until the edges turn golden brown.

8. Allow the rolls to cool in the pan for 2 to 3 minutes.

9. Just before serving, brush the tops of the rolls with melted butter.

SUNFLOWER SEED BREAD

COOK TIME: 1 HOUR | MAKES: 1

INGREDIENTS:

- 1 ½ cups sunflower seeds
- 1 cup sliced almonds
- Non-stick cooking spray
- 1 ¾ cups old-fashioned rolled oats
- ¼ cup whole flaxseeds
- 4 tbsp powdered psyllium husk
- 1 ½ cups water
- 4 tbsp coconut oil, melted and cooled
- 2 tbsp organic honey
- ¾ tsp fine salt

DIRECTIONS:

1. Preheat the oven to 350°F or 180°C. Coat a loaf pan with non-stick cooking spray.

2. Put the sunflower seeds and sliced almonds on the rimmed baking sheet and bake for 10 to 12 minutes, stirring occasionally until lightly browned.

3. Transfer the toasted nut-seed mixture into a large mixing bowl and allow it to cool slightly. Add the rolled oats, flaxseeds, and powdered psyllium.

4. In a separate mixing bowl, add water, melted coconut oil, organic honey, and fine salt, and whisk to combine. Use a silicone spatula to mix the water mixture into the nut-seed mixture until fully incorporated.

5. Transfer the dough mixture to the prepared pan. Use wet hands to press the dough into the corners and smooth the top.

6. Cover loosely with a damp kitchen towel and allow it to rest for 2 hours at room temperature.

7. Preheat the oven to 350°F or 180°C. Remove the towel and bake the loaf for 20 minutes.

8. Remove the bread loaf from the pan and place it on a wire rack set inside a rimmed baking pan. Bake the loaf for 35 to 45 minutes until deep golden brown and the loaf sounds hollow when tapped.

9. Allow the loaf to cool for 2 hours, then serve.

MEDITERRANEAN LOAF

COOK TIME: 2 HOURS | MAKES: 1

INGREDIENTS:

- Non-stick cooking spray
- 1½ cups warm water
- 3 large eggs, beaten
- 3 tbsp sunflower oil
- 2 tsp lime juice
- 2 ⅔ cups Bob's Red Mill gluten-free 1-to-1 baking flour
- 1 ⅓ cups gluten-free millet flour
- ½ cup milk powder
- 1 pkt fast rising instant yeast
- 3 tbsp powdered psyllium husk
- 3 tbsp granulated sugar
- 1 tsp fine salt
- ¾ tsp baking soda
- 1½ cups pitted black olives, rinsed, and chopped

DIRECTIONS:

1. In a medium mixing bowl, add the warm water, beaten eggs, 2 tablespoons sunflower oil, and lime juice, and mix to combine.

2. In a stand mixer fitted with the hook attachment, add the gluten-free flour, millet flour, milk powder, instant yeast, psyllium, granulated sugar, fine salt, and baking soda, and mix until combined. Add the water mixture and mix for 2 minutes for the dough to come together, scraping down the sides as needed.

3. Increase speed to medium and beat for 6 minutes until sticky and uniform. Mix in the chopped olives.

4. Spray a baking sheet with non-stick cooking spray.

5. Transfer the dough onto the prepared baking sheet and shape it into a ball with your wet hands.

6. Using a sharp knife, cut an X shape across the top of the dough.

7. Spray the dough with water. Cover loosely with a damp kitchen towel and let it rise for 1½ hours at room temperature.

8. Preheat the oven to 325°F or 170°C. Remove the kitchen towel and brush the dough with the remaining sunflower oil.

9. Bake for 2 hours or until the top of the bread is dark golden brown and the loaf sounds hollow when tapped.

10. Remove the loaf from the baking sheet, and transfer it to a wire rack. Allow the bread to cool for 2 hours before serving.

CORN LOAF

COOK TIME: 25 MIN | SERVES: 12

INGREDIENTS:

- Non-stick cooking spray
- 1½ cups fat-free milk
- 1½ tbsp white vinegar
- 1½ cups gluten-free cornmeal
- 1 cup Bob's Red Mill gluten-free 1-to-1 baking flour
- 1 tsp granulated sugar
- ½ tsp baking soda
- 2 tsp baking powder
- 1 tsp fine salt
- ½ cup gluten-free butter spread, melted
- 2 large eggs, beaten

DIRECTIONS:

1. Preheat the oven to 400°F or 200°C. Coat a cast-iron pan with nonstick cooking spray.

2. In a small mixing bowl, combine the fat-free milk and white vinegar and allow to sit for 2 minutes to make buttermilk.

3. In a large-sized mixing bowl, add the cornmeal, gluten-free flour, granulated sugar, baking soda, baking powder, and fine salt, and mix to combine.

4. Add the melted butter, beaten eggs, and the milk mixture, and mix until fully combined.

5. Pour the batter into the prepared cast-iron pan and smooth the top of the batter.

6. Bake for 20–25 minutes or until golden brown and a toothpick inserted comes out clean.

7. Allow to cool for 5 minutes before cutting. Serve warm.

APPLESAUCE LOAF

COOK TIME: 50 MIN | SERVES: 8

INGREDIENTS:

- Nonstick cooking spray
- 1 ½ cups applesauce
- ⅓ cup coconut oil, melted
- 2 large eggs, beaten
- ½ cup granulated sugar
- 1 tsp vanilla extract
- ½ tsp xanthan gum
- 1½ cups Bob's Red Mill gluten-free 1-to-1 baking flour
- 1 tsp baking soda
- ½ tsp baking powder
- 1 tbsp ground cinnamon
- ⅛ tsp fine salt
- 1 cup unsweetened soy milk

DIRECTIONS:

1. Preheat to oven to 350°F or 180°C. Coat a long loaf pan with nonstick cooking spray.

2. In a mixing bowl, add the applesauce, melted coconut oil, beaten eggs, granulated sugar, and vanilla extract, and mix to combine.

3. Add the xanthan gum, gluten-free flour, baking soda, baking powder, ground cinnamon, and fine salt, and mix until fully combined.

4. Add the soy milk and mix until smooth. Pour the batter into a prepared loaf pan.

5. Bake for 50 minutes to 1 hour or until a toothpick inserted comes out clean.

6. Allow the bread to cool for 3–5 minutes before removing it from the pan and slicing.

GARLIC PITA BREAD

COOK TIME: 10 MIN | SERVES: 4

INGREDIENTS:

- Non-stick cooking spray
- 1 ¾ cups Bob's Red Mill gluten-free 1-to-1 baking flour
- ½ tsp fine salt
- 1 tsp granulated sugar
- 1 packet fast-rising instant yeast
- ½ cup low-fat milk
- 3 tbsp butter, softened
- 2 tsp garlic, crushed
- 1 large egg, room temperature
- 1 tbsp organic honey
- ½ tsp apple cider vinegar

DIRECTIONS:

1. Preheat the oven to 450°F or 230°C.

2. Using a stand mixer fitted with a dough hook, add the gluten-free flour, fine salt, and granulated sugar, and mix to combine.

3. Make a well in the middle of the flour, then add the fast-rising yeast.

4. Microwave the low-fat milk for 45 seconds until warm and pour it over the yeast.

5. Add the softened butter, crushed garlic, egg, organic honey, and apple cider vinegar, and mix for 2 minutes until combined.

6. Coat a large baking sheet with cooking spray. Place the dough on the baking sheet and flatten it into a rectangle.

7. Bake for 12 minutes until the edges look crisp, but the center is still doughy.

CHEDDAR SALTINES

COOK TIME: 15 MIN | MAKES: 8

INGREDIENTS:

- 1 cup Bob's Red Mill gluten-free 1-to-1 baking flour
- 1 cup shredded mild cheddar cheese
- 4 ½ tbsp unsalted butter, softened
- Non-stick cooking spray
- 1 tbsp fine salt

DIRECTIONS:

1. In a food processor, add the flour, cheddar cheese, and softened butter. Process for 1 to 2 minutes until a dough forms.

2. Wrap the dough in plastic wrap and refrigerate for 10 minutes to chill.

3. Preheat the oven to 350°F or 180°C. Spray a baking sheet with non-stick cooking spray and dust the rolling pin with flour.

4. Roll out the dough onto the baking sheet into a 4-by-8-inch rectangle, about 1 inch thick. Cut the dough into 8 squares and sprinkle with fine salt.

5. Bake for 13 to 15 minutes until the edge of the dough starts to turn a golden color.

6. Remove from the oven and allow it to cool in the pan for 1 to 2 minutes.

7. Transfer to a wire rack to cool completely.

FRENCH CRANBERRY BREAD

COOK TIME: 1 HOUR | MAKES: 1

INGREDIENTS:

- 2 cups whole milk, heated
- 4 tsp fast-rising instant yeast
- 2 tbsp plus 1 tsp granulated sugar
- 2 large eggs, beaten
- 3 ⅓ cups Bob's Red Mill gluten-free 1-to-1 baking flour
- 2 ½ tbsp powdered psyllium husk

- 1 ½ tsp fine salt
- ¾ tsp baking soda
- 1 cup pecan nuts, chopped
- ½ cup dried cranberries
- Parchment paper
- Non-stick cooking spray

DIRECTIONS:

1. In a medium mixing bowl, add the warm milk, instant yeast, and 1 teaspoon of granulated sugar, and allow to sit for 5 minutes until foamy. Add the beaten eggs and mix.

2. Using a stand mixer fitted with a paddle attachment, add the flour, psyllium husk, fine salt, baking soda, and remaining 2 tablespoons of sugar, and mix on low speed for 2 minutes until combined.

3. Add the yeast mixture and mix for 2 minutes until combined, scrape the sides of the bowl as needed. Increase the speed to medium and beat for 7 minutes until sticky and uniform. Reduce the speed to low, add chopped pecan nuts and dried cranberries, and mix for 30 to 60 seconds until incorporated.

4. Coat a sheet of parchment paper with non-stick cooking spray. Transfer the dough onto the prepared parchment.

5. Use wet hands to shape the dough into a ball, then place the dough with the parchment into an 8-inch, cast-iron skillet.

6. Use a knife, to cut a deep X across the top of the dough. Cover loosely with a damp kitchen towel, and place the skillet in the warmed oven, allow it to rise for 10 minutes.

7. Remove the cast-iron skillet from the oven and let sit on the counter for 20 minutes. Meanwhile, place a baking stone or baking pan on the oven rack and heat the oven to 400°F or 200°C.

8. Remove the towel and spray the loaf with water. Reduce oven temperature to 350°F or 180°C and place the cast-iron skillet on the baking stone or baking pan.

9. Bake for 55 minutes to 1 ¼ hours until the top of the bread is well browned, and the loaf sounds hollow when tapped.

10. Being careful of the hot skillet handle, remove it from the oven and place the bread onto a wire rack. Allow it to cool for 3 hours before serving.

Tip: to help the proofing of the dough, first heat the oven to 275°F or 140°C for 10 minutes, then turn it off. This will act as a warm proofing box for the dough. Start with step 2 once the oven has been turned off.

PARMESAN LOAF

COOK TIME: 45 MIN | MAKES: 1

INGREDIENTS:

- Non-stick cooking spray
- 1 cup Parmesan cheese, grated
- 2 ¾ cups Bob's Red Mill gluten-free 1-to-1 baking flour
- 1 tbsp baking powder
- ¼ tsp baking soda
- ½ tsp fine salt
- ¼ tsp ground white pepper
- ½ tsp smoked paprika
- 1 cup gouda cheese, cut into small cubes
- 1 ¼ cups sour cream
- 3 tbsp unsalted butter, melted and cooled
- 2 large eggs, lightly beaten

DIRECTIONS:

1. Preheat the oven to 350°F or 180°C. Coat a loaf pan with non-stick cooking spray, and sprinkle half of the Parmesan cheese evenly at the bottom of the pan.

2. In a large mixing bowl, add the flour, baking powder, baking soda, fine salt, ground white pepper, and smoked paprika, and mix to combine.

3. Add the cut gouda cheese, breaking it up with your fingers until coated with the flour mixture.

4. In a separate mixing bowl, add the sour cream, melted butter and beaten eggs, and whisk until smooth. Use a silicone spatula to stir the sour cream mixture into the flour mixture until fully combined.

5. Scrape the batter into the prepared pan, smooth the top, and sprinkle the remaining Parmesan cheese evenly over the loaf.

6. Bake for 40 to 45 minutes until deep golden brown and a toothpick inserted comes out clean.

7. Transfer to a wire rack and let the bread cool in the pan for 10 minutes. Remove the loaf and allow it to cool on the rack for 1 hour before serving.

CINNAMON RING ROLLS

COOK TIME: 20 MIN | MAKES: 8

INGREDIENTS:

- Non-stick cooking spray
- Parchment paper
- 2 ¼ cups plus 1 tbsp water, warmed
- 1 packet fast-rising instant yeast
- 1 tbsp sugar
- 3 ½ cups Bob's Red Mill gluten-free 1-to-1 baking flour
- ½ tsp xanthan gum
- 3 tbsp psyllium husk powder

- 2 tsp baking powder
- 1 ½ tsp fine salt
- 1 tbsp light brown sugar
- 1 tsp ground cinnamon
- 1 cup unsalted butter, melted and cooled
- 1 tsp white vinegar
- ¼ cup organic honey
- 1 egg white

DIRECTIONS:

1. Preheat the oven to 275°F or 140°C for 15 minutes, and turn it off. Coat an ovenproof safe bowl with non-stick cooking spray, and set aside.

2. Use a stand mixer fitted with a dough hook, add the warm water, instant yeast, and sugar, mix, and allow it to stand for 5 minutes until foamy. Add the gluten-free flour, xanthan gum, psyllium husk powder, baking powder, fine salt, light brown sugar, and ground cinnamon mix until fully combined.

3. Add the melted butter and white vinegar and beat on low speed for 2 minutes. Increase the speed to medium and knead for 8 minutes.

4. Place the dough inside the prepared ovenproof safe bowl. Cover the bowl with a damp kitchen towel. Allow the dough to rise for 30 minutes in the warm oven.

5. Line a baking pan with parchment paper. Place the dough onto the parchment paper and cut it into eight pieces. Roll each piece into a ball. Press your finger through the center of each ball to make a hole. Cover the ring shapes rolls with a kitchen towel and allow them to rise for 10 minutes on the counter.

6. Preheat the oven to 425°F or 220°C.

7. Fill a large stockpot with 2 quarts water. Add in the organic honey and whisk. Allow the water to boil, then reduce heat to medium. Drop the rolls in the water one at a time. Cook the rolls for 30 seconds on each side. Remove with a slotted spoon and return boiled rolls onto the baking pan.

8. In a small mixing bowl, add the egg white and 1 tablespoon water, and whisk to combine.

9. Brush the tops and sides of the rolls with the egg wash. Bake for 7 minutes, rotate the pan and bake for another 8 minutes until golden brown.

10. Remove from the oven and allow the rolls to cool on the baking sheet for 20 minutes before serving.

GARLIC ROSEMARY GRISSINI

COOK TIME: 15 MIN | MAKES: 16

INGREDIENTS:

- Non-stick cooking spray
- 2 ½ cups plus 1 tbsp Bob's Red Mill gluten-free 1-to-1 baking flour
- 1 packet fast-rising instant yeast
- ½ tsp xanthan gum
- 1 tbsp baking powder
- 1 tsp fine salt
- ¼ tsp garlic powder

- 1 tbsp honey
- 1½ cups warm water
- ½ cup plus 2 tsp olive oil, divided
- 1 tsp apple cider vinegar
- 3 tbsp unsalted butter
- 1 tsp garlic, minced
- ½ tsp rosemary, chopped

DIRECTIONS:

1. In the stand mixer bowl, add the gluten-free flour, instant yeast, xanthan gum, baking powder, fine salt, and garlic powder, and mix to combine. Add the honey into the bowl with the warm water, and mix to dissolve.

2. Add the honey water into the flour mixture and mix with the dough hook attachment on low.

3. Add ½ cup of olive oil and apple cider vinegar into the dough mixture and mix for 5 minutes on medium speed.

4. Coat a baking pan with non-stick cooking spray. Pour the remaining 2 teaspoons of olive oil into a sealable plastic bag or piping bag and spread around until it's coated.

5. Put the dough into the bag toward one of the bottom corners. Cut a piece off the corner of the bag. Push the dough toward the cut corner.

6. Pipe the dough on the prepared baking pan to form the length of a breadstick, Repeat the piping of the dough into breadstick shapes until all dough is used. Cover with a kitchen towel and put it in a warm place to rise for 20 minutes.

7. Preheat the oven to 425°F or 220°C.

8. In a small microwave-safe bowl, add the unsalted butter, minced garlic and chopped rosemary, and microwave for 30 seconds, or until the butter has melted.

9. Bake the breadsticks for 15 minutes until golden brown. Brush the tops with melted rosemary garlic butter. Allow to cool for 2 minutes, serve warm.

ALLSPICE CRACKERS

COOK TIME: 15 MIN | MAKES: 24

INGREDIENTS:

- Parchment paper
- 2 ¼ cups almond flour
- ½ cup light brown sugar
- 1 tsp baking powder
- 1 tsp ground allspice
- ½ tsp ground cinnamon
- ½ tsp fine salt
- 1 large egg, beaten
- 3 tbsp maple syrup
- 3 tbsp coconut oil, melted

DIRECTIONS:

1. Preheat the oven to 325°F or 170°C. Line a large baking pan with parchment paper.

2. In a large mixing bowl, add the almond flour, light brown sugar, baking powder, allspice, ground cinnamon, and fine salt, and mix to combine. Add the beaten egg, maple syrup, and melted coconut oil, and mix until fully incorporated. Refrigerate for 40 minutes.

3. Place the dough on the baking pan and place another sheet of parchment paper or a silicone mat on top of the dough.

4. Use a rolling pin to roll the dough into a rectangle, about 1/8 inch thick.

5. Remove the top sheet of parchment paper and cut the dough into equal-size rectangles or squares. Bake for 12 to 15 minutes, or until the edges turn golden but the centers are still soft.

6. Remove from the oven and allow the crackers to cool for 5 minutes in the baking pan before transferring them to a wire rack to cool completely.

Substitution tip: you can replace the coconut oil with butter. The measurements stay the same.

PASTA & NOODLES

GROUND CHICKEN TAGLIATELLE

COOK TIME: 40 MIN | SERVES: 4

INGREDIENTS:

- 1 lb. 85 lean ground chicken
- 2 tbsp water
- 1 tsp fine salt, divided
- 1 tsp ground black pepper, divided
- ½ tsp baking soda
- 4 oz white mushrooms, quartered
- 1 tbsp canola oil
- 1 yellow onion, finely chopped

- 1½ tbsp garlic, minced
- 1 tbsp tomato paste
- ¼ cup fresh basil, chopped
- ¼ tsp smoked paprika
- 1 (28oz) can tomato puree
- 1 (14.5oz) can diced tomatoes, drained
- ¼ cup grated Parmesan cheese, plus extra for serving
- 9 oz gluten-free rice egg tagliatelle

DIRECTIONS:

1. In a medium mixing bowl, add the ground chicken, water, ½ teaspoon of fine salt, ½ teaspoon of ground black pepper, and baking soda, and mix until fully combined.

2. In a food processor, add the quartered mushrooms and pulse 8 times, or until finely chopped.

3. Heat the canola oil in a large, heavy-bottom pan over medium heat until hot. Add the finely chopped mushrooms and chopped onion and cook for 8 to 10 minutes until the vegetables are brown.

4. Add the minced garlic, tomato paste, chopped basil and smoked paprika, and cook for 30 seconds until fragrant.

5. Add the tomato puree, diced tomatoes, ½ teaspoon of fine salt, and ½ teaspoon of ground black pepper, mix and allow to simmer.

6. Add the ground chicken mixture and cook for 30 minutes, breaking it up with a fork until cooked through and the sauce has thickened.

7. Add the grated Parmesan and season with fine salt and ground black pepper to taste.

8. Meanwhile, cook the tagliatelle according to the package instructions. Reserve ½ cup of the cooking water, then drain the pasta and return it to the pot.

9. Add the meat sauce to the pasta and toss to coat.

10. Add reserved cooking water as needed to adjust consistency. Serve with a sprinkle of Parmesan.

JAPANESE AUBERGINE NOODLES

COOK TIME: 38 MIN | SERVES: 4

INGREDIENTS:

- 4 tbsp canola oil, divided
- 2 lb. aubergines, cut into pieces
- 4 tbsp gluten-free tamari
- 4 tbsp light brown sugar
- 3 tbsp sesame oil
- 4 tsp Japanese rice wine
- 1 tbsp Asian chili-garlic sauce
- 1 tbsp gluten-free oyster sauce
- 8 oz gluten-free buckwheat noodles
- ¾ cup fresh parsley, chopped
- 3 tsp sesame seeds, toasted

DIRECTIONS:

1. Preheat the oven to 450°F or 230°C. Line a baking sheet with aluminum foil and brush with 1 tablespoon canola oil.

2. In a large mixing bowl, add the aubergine pieces, the remaining 3 tablespoons canola oil and 1 tablespoon of tamari, and toss to coat. Spread the coated aubergine pieces onto the prepared baking sheet. Roast for 25 to 30 minutes, mixing halfway until well browned and tender.

3. In a small stockpot, add the remaining 3 tablespoons tamari, light brown sugar, sesame oil, rice wine, chili-garlic sauce, oyster sauce, and whisk to combine. Cook for 1 minute, over medium heat until the sugar has dissolved, and set aside.

4. Fill a large stockpot with water and allow it to boil. Add the buckwheat noodles and cook for 8 minutes, stirring often until tender.

5. Reserve ½ cup of the cooking water, drain the noodles and return them to the pot.

6. Add the sauce and roasted aubergines, and toss to combine. Add the reserved cooking water as needed to adjust the consistency.

7. Sprinkle individual portions with chopped parsley and toasted sesame seeds and serve.

RICOTTA LASAGNA

COOK TIME: 25 MIN | SERVES: 4

INGREDIENTS:

- 1 (16oz) container ricotta cheese
- 1 large egg, whisked
- 1 tsp Italian seasoning
- 2 cups shredded mozzarella cheese
- 4 cups shredded Italian cheese blend, divided
- 2 (15oz) cans tomato sauce
- 1 (9oz) package oven-ready, gluten-free lasagna noodles
- 2 cups fresh basil leaves, finely chopped

DIRECTIONS:

1. Preheat the oven to 375°F or 190°C.

2. In a medium mixing bowl, add the ricotta cheese, whisked egg, Italian seasoning, shredded mozzarella, 1½ cups of Italian cheese blend, and mix to combine.

3. Cover the bottom of a large square or rectangular glass baking dish with 1 cup of tomato sauce.

4. Place a layer of lasagna noodles over the sauce, and top with 1 cup of tomato sauce. Spread to cover the noodles.

5. Cover the tomato sauce with ½ cup of the ricotta cheese mixture and sprinkle chopped fresh basil.

6. Repeat, building two more layers with the noodles, tomato sauce, ricotta cheese mixture, and chopped basil as described in steps 4 and 5. Make sure to end with the cheese mixture and chopped basil.

7. Bake for 25 minutes, uncovered, or until the cheese is browned and bubbling. Serve hot.

BROCCOLI ROTINI PASTA

COOK TIME: 30 MIN | SERVES: 4

INGREDIENTS:

- 2 tbsp canola oil
- 1 small head broccoli, cored and cut into small florets
- 1 yellow onion, sliced
- 2 ½ tsp fine salt, divided
- Ground black pepper
- ¼ cup water
- ½ cup pine nuts, chopped
- 6 tbsp unsalted butter
- 1 tbsp garlic, minced
- ¾ tsp ground cumin
- ¾ tsp ground ginger
- ¼ tsp cayenne pepper
- 3 cups baby spinach
- ¾ tsp lime juice
- 8.8 oz chickpea Rotini Pasta

DIRECTIONS:

1. In a heavy bottom frying pan over medium heat, heat the canola oil until hot.

2. Add the broccoli florets, sliced onion, and 1/4 teaspoon fine salt and cook for 12 to 15 minutes, stirring occasionally until well browned.

3. Add water to the pan, cover, and continue to cook for 2 minutes until the broccoli is tender. Transfer to a bowl and set aside.

4. Dry the pan with paper towels. Add the pine nuts and toast over medium heat for 3 to 5 minutes, shaking frequently until fragrant and lightly browned.

5. Add the butter, and cook for 1 to 2 minutes, swirling occasionally until the butter has browned.

6. Turn off the heat, add the minced garlic, ground cumin, ground ginger, cayenne pepper, and cook for 1 minute, swirling the pan until garlic and spices are fragrant.

7. Mix in the broccoli and onion mixture, baby spinach, lime juice, and 1/4 teaspoon fine salt, cover, and let sit for 2 minutes until spinach is wilted.

8. Fill a large stockpot with water and allow to boil. Add the pasta and 2 teaspoons fine salt and cook for 8 minutes, stirring occasionally until al dente. Reserve ½ cup of the cooking water, then drain the pasta and return it to the pot.

9. Add the broccoli sauce, and toss to combine, season with fine salt and ground black pepper to taste. Add the remaining cooking water as needed to adjust consistency. Serve warm.

SPAGHETTI SQUASH

COOK TIME: 40 MIN | SERVES: 2

INGREDIENTS:

- 1 spaghetti squash
- 1 tsp olive oil
- ½ tsp fine salt
- ½ tsp ground black pepper

DIRECTIONS:

1. Preheat the oven to 400°F or 200°C. Line a baking pan with aluminum foil.

2. Cut the spaghetti squash in half lengthwise, and discard the seeds. Drizzle the olive oil over the squash and season with fine salt and ground black pepper.

3. Place the spaghetti squash cut side down on the prepared baking sheet. Using a fork, poke holes all over the skin. Roast for 30 to 40 minutes until lightly browned on the outside and fork-tender.

4. Allow the spaghetti squash to cool down enough for you to handle.

5. Use a fork to scrape the flesh and fluff the strands from the sides of the squash. Serve with your choice of protein or use it in place of a spaghetti dish.

Tip: the cooking time may vary depending on the size of the spaghetti squash. Alternatively, you can purchase a 12 oz bag of butternut squash spirals to cut down cooking time.

CHEESY MACARONI

COOK TIME: 15 MIN | SERVES: 4

INGREDIENTS:

- 2 tbsp unsalted butter
- 1 tbsp canola oil
- ½ cup gluten-free natural smoked chorizo, chopped
- 16 oz gluten-free brown rice elbow macaroni
- 2 cups gluten-free Cheese Sauce
- 2 spring onions, green parts, thinly sliced
- 1 cup shredded fiesta cheese blend

DIRECTIONS:

1. Preheat the broiler to high. Coat a deep casserole dish with unsalted butter.

2. In a heavy bottom pan over high heat, add the canola oil until hot. Add the chopped chorizo and cook for 8 minutes, or until browned. Set aside.

3. Bring a large stockpot of salted water to a boil over high heat. Cook the pasta for 10 to 18 minutes, or until al dente. Drain and return to the pot.

4. Pour the cheese sauce over the macaroni and mix to combine.

5. Add the fried chorizo and sliced spring onion, and mix to combine.

6. Transfer the macaroni mixture into the prepared casserole dish and top with the shredded fiesta cheese blend.

7. Broil for 1 to 3 minutes, or until the cheese is brown and bubbling.

Tip: alternatively, you can make your own cheese sauce by adding 4 tbsp butter, into a medium-sized stockpot until melted. Remove from the heat and add in 4 tbsp gluten-free flour, whisk to combine. Season with salt and pepper to taste. Slowly whisk in 2 cups of whole milk until no lumps remain. Add in 1 cup of shredded fiesta cheese blend. Keep whisking on medium heat until the sauce has thickened. Pour over pasta.

PARMESAN SPINACH PENNE

COOK TIME: 22 MIN | SERVES: 4

INGREDIENTS:

- 2 tbsp canola oil
- 1 lb. spinach, sliced thinly and washed
- 1½ tbsp garlic, minced
- 1 tsp lime zest, grated
- 1½ tsp oregano, chopped
- 1 lb. green beans, ends trimmed and cut in half
- ½ cup white cooking wine
- 1 cup heavy whipping cream
- Fine salt
- Ground black pepper
- ¾ cup shelled edamame, cooked
- 1 cup Parmesan cheese, grated and divided
- 8 oz gluten-free Banza penne pasta
- 2 tbsp fresh basil, chopped
- 8 cups water

DIRECTIONS:

1. In a heavy bottom pan over medium heat, heat the canola oil until hot. Add the sliced spinach and cook for 5 to 7 minutes, or until softened.

2. Add the minced garlic, lime zest and chopped oregano, and cook for 30 seconds. until fragrant.

3. Add the cut green beans and white cooking wine, bring to simmer, and cook for 3 minutes until the green beans are tender. Add in heavy whipping cream, fine salt and ground black pepper to taste and bring to simmer.

4. Cook for 2 minutes until the sauce has thickened. Turn off the heat, mix in the cooked edamame, grated Parmesan, and let sit, covered until the edamame is heated through.

5. In a large stockpot, add the water and fine salt, and allow to boil. Add the penne pasta and cook for 8 to 10 minutes, stirring occasionally until al dente. Reserve ½ cup of the cooking water, then drain the pasta and return it to the pot.

6. Add the spinach sauce and mix to combine. Season with fine salt and ground black pepper to taste. Add reserved cooking water as needed to adjust consistency.

7. Sprinkle with chopped basil and serve, garnished with the remaining Parmesan cheese.

PORK CHORIZO PASTA

COOK TIME: 46 MIN | SERVES: 4

INGREDIENTS:

- 1 tbsp vegetable oil
- 1 red onion, chopped fine
- 1 green bell pepper, stemmed, seeded, and chopped into small cubes
- 2 tbsp tomato paste
- 4 ½ tsp garlic, minced
- 2 tsp minced fresh Marjoram or 1 tsp dried
- 1 lb. El Mexicano Pork Chorizo, casing removed
- ½ cup red cooking wine
- 1 (28 oz) can crushed tomatoes
- 12 oz Jovial Pasta Shells
- Fine salt
- Ground black pepper
- 2 tbsp fresh parsley, finely chopped
- Parmesan cheese, grated

DIRECTIONS:

1. In a Dutch oven, heat vegetable oil over medium heat until hot. Add the chopped onion and cubed bell pepper and fry for 6 minutes until softened.

2. Add the tomato paste, minced garlic, and marjoram to the onion mixture and cook for 1 minute until fragrant. Add the chorizo and cook for 7 minutes—breaking it up with a fork—and no longer pink.

3. Pour the red wine into the chorizo mixture, scraping up any browned bits, and let it simmer for 2 minutes until the liquid has thickened.

4. Add the crushed tomatoes, and let it simmer for 30 minutes until the sauce has thickened.

5. In a large stockpot, add water and bring to a boil. Add the pasta shells along with 1 tablespoon fine salt, stirring often until al dente.

6. Set aside ½ cup of the cooking water, drain the pasta and return it to the pot. Add the chorizo sauce and chopped parsley to the pasta, and mix to combine, season with fine salt and ground black pepper for taste.

7. Add the reserved cooking water to the pasta mixture as needed to adjust consistency. Serve with grated Parmesan cheese.

TURKEY VEGGIE PASTA

COOK TIME: 31 MIN | SERVES: 4

INGREDIENTS:

- 1 (12oz) box gluten-free Cavatappi pasta
- ½ cup canola oil, divided
- 2 (6 oz) boneless, skinless turkey breast fillets
- ½ tsp fine salt
- ¼ tsp ground black pepper
- 1 tsp garlic, minced
- 1 small red onion, sliced
- 1 large carrot, peeled and julienned
- 1 red bell pepper, seeded julienned
- 1 fresh chayote squash, halved and thinly sliced
- 1 large zucchini, halved and sliced
- 1 cup cherry tomatoes, halved
- 1 tbsp Italian seasoning blend
- 1 tbsp lemon juice

DIRECTIONS:

1. Cook the Cavatappi pasta according to the package directions.

2. Add 2 tablespoons of canola oil into a large heavy bottom frying pan over medium heat.

3. Season the turkey breasts with fine salt and ground black pepper. Cook for 6 to 7 minutes on each side until golden brown and cooked through. Remove from the pan and let it rest for 10 minutes before slicing.

4. Add the remaining canola oil and minced garlic to the pan and sauté for 20 seconds until fragrant.

5. Add the sliced onion, julienned carrots and julienned bell pepper, and sauté for 5 minutes. Add the thinly sliced chayote and zucchini to the pan and sauté for 2 minutes until softened.

6. Add the halved tomatoes, Italian seasoning blend, and lemon juice, and sauté for 2 minutes.

7. In a large bowl, add the cooked pasta and vegetable mixture, and toss to combine. Top with the sliced turkey and serve.

SHRIMP CHINESE NOODLES

COOK TIME: 30 MIN | SERVES: 4

INGREDIENTS:

- 8 oz dried rice vermicelli
- 1 lb. large shrimps, peeled, deveined, and tails removed
- 3 tsp curry powder, mild
- ⅛ tsp granulated sugar
- 2 tbsp canola oil
- 6 yellow onions, sliced thin
- 2 green bell peppers, stemmed, seeded, and cut into strips
- 3 tsp garlic, minced
- 1 cup chicken broth
- ⅓ cup gluten-free tamari
- 1 tbsp sherry cooking wine
- 1 tsp mild sweet chili sauce
- 1 (16 oz) can butter beans, drained and rinsed
- ½ cup fresh parsley, minced

DIRECTIONS:

1. Soak the noodles in a bowl with very hot tap water for 20 minutes until softened, pliable, and limp but not fully tender, drain. Pat the shrimps dry with paper towels.

2. In a large bowl, add the dried shrimps, ½ teaspoon curry powder and granulated sugar, and toss to combine.

3. Heat 1 tablespoon of canola oil in a Dutch oven over high heat until smoking. Add the shrimps in a single layer and cook for 1 to 2 minutes until beginning to brown. Flip the shrimp and continue to cook for 30 seconds until spotty brown and just pink around the edges. Transfer the shrimp into a clean bowl.

4. Heat the remaining 1 tablespoon of canola oil to the Dutch oven pot over medium heat until shimmering. Add the sliced onions, bell pepper strips, and the remaining 2½ teaspoons curry powder and cook for 3 to 5 minutes until the vegetables have softened. Add the minced garlic and cook for 40 seconds.

5. Add the drained noodles, shrimp with the accumulated juices, chicken broth, tamari, sherry cooking wine and sweet chili sauce, and cook for 2 to 3 minutes, tossing gently to coat the noodles.

6. Add the rinsed butter beans and minced parsley. Serve warm.

SPICY TEMPEH NOODLES

COOK TIME: 20 MIN | SERVES: 4

INGREDIENTS:

- 12 oz dried gluten-free rice noodles
- 14 oz tempeh, cut into cubes
- 6–8 Jalapeño chiles, stemmed and seeded
- 2 tbsp garlic, minced
- 2 small red onions, peeled
- 2 cups chicken broth
- ¼ cup gluten-free tamari
- ¼ cup light brown sugar
- 3 tbsp lime juice
- ½ cup cornstarch
- Fine salt
- Ground black pepper
- 7 tbsp canola oil
- 6 oz sugar snap peas, strings removed
- 1 red bell pepper, stemmed, seeded, cut into large squares
- 2 cups fresh basil leaves, chopped

DIRECTIONS:

1. Cover noodles with hot tap water in large bowl and stir to separate. Let the noodles soak for 35 to 40 minutes until softened, pliable, and limp but not fully tender, drain.

2. Drain the tempeh for 20 minutes, then pat dry with paper towels.

3. In a food processor, add the Jalapeño chiles, minced garlic, and red onions, and pulse into a smooth paste.

4. In a medium bowl, add the chicken broth, tamari, light brown sugar and lime juice, and whisk to combine.

5. Preheat the oven to 275°F or 140°C.

6. In a shallow dish spread the cornstarch. Season the tempeh with fine salt and ground black pepper to taste, then dredge it in the cornstarch and transfer to a separate plate.

7. Heat 3 tablespoons of canola oil in a nonstick frying pan over medium heat until smoking.

8. Fry the tempeh for 4 minutes on each side until all the sides are crispy and brown, then transfer onto a paper, towel–lined plate.

9. Clean the pan with paper towels and add 1 tablespoon of canola oil over high heat until smoking.

10. Add snap peas and cut bell pepper, and cook for 3 to 5 minutes, stirring often until vegetables are tender and beginning to brown, then transfer into a bowl.

11. Add the remaining canola oil into a now-empty pan over medium heat until shimmering.

12. Add the chile mixture and cook for 3 to 5 minutes until the moisture evaporates, and the color deepens. Add the drained noodles and broth mixture and cook for 5 to 10 minutes, tossing gently until the sauce has thickened, and the noodles are well coated.

13. Add the cooked vegetables and chopped basil, and cook for 1 minute, stirring occasionally. Divide into serving bowls and top each with crispy tempeh and serve.

Courgette Noodles

COOK TIME: 11 MIN | SERVES: 4

INGREDIENTS:

- 1 tbsp canola oil
- ½ tsp garlic, minced
- 1 (12 oz) bag frozen Green Giant courgette spirals

DIRECTIONS:

1. Put the canola oil into a large, heavy-bottom pan and allow it to become hot.

2. Add the minced garlic and fry for 1 minute until fragrant.

3. Add the frozen courgette spirals, cover with a lid, and allow to cook for 10 minutes, stirring occasionally.

4. Drain the excess liquid and serve with your choice of meat.

Tip: alternatively, you can spiral fresh courgettes by using a spiral cutter or cutting the courgettes lengthwise into ribbons and then julienning them.

CLASSIC COMFORT FOODS

TILAPIA & FRIES

COOK TIME: 35 MIN | SERVES: 4

INGREDIENTS:

- 2 large Russet potatoes, scrubbed, and cut into wide spears
- 2 tbsp sunflower oil
- ½ tsp fine salt, divided
- 1½ cups gluten-free breadcrumbs
- ¼ tsp garlic powder
- ¼ tsp onion powder
- ½ tsp smoked paprika
- 2 large eggs
- 4 tilapia fillets, boneless and skinless

DIRECTIONS:

1. Preheat the oven to 425°F or 220°C. Line a rimmed baking pan with aluminum foil.

2. Spread the potato spears on the pan and drizzle with the sunflower oil. Toss to coat. Season the spears with 1/4 teaspoon of fine salt. Bake for 15 minutes.

3. In a shallow dish, add the breadcrumbs, the remaining 1/4 teaspoon fine salt, garlic powder, onion powder and smoked paprika, and mix to combine.

4. In another shallow dish, add the eggs and whisk until foamy.

5. Coat the tilapia fillets in the seasoned breadcrumb mixture, then dip them into the whisked egg, and then coat with breadcrumbs. Repeat with the remaining tilapia fillets.

6. Remove the pan from the oven and place the crumbed tilapia fillets on top of the potatoes spaced apart. Bake for 10 minutes more, or until the fish is cooked through and the potatoes have browned.

MUSHROOM PIZZA

COOK TIME: 15 MIN | SERVES: 2

INGREDIENTS:

For the crust
- 1 ½ tsp granulated sugar
- ⅓ cup warm water
- 2 ¼ tsp fast rising instant yeast
- 1 cup Bob's Red Mill gluten-free 1-to-1 baking flour
- ¾ cup tapioca flour
- ¾ tsp fine salt
- 1 large egg white
- 1 ½ tsp apple cider vinegar
- ¼ cup potato starch
- 2 tbsp canola oil

For the topping
- 1 cup tomato sauce
- 1 tsp oregano, finely chopped
- ½ tsp garlic, minced
- 1 tbsp unsalted butter
- 1 cup shiitake mushrooms, sliced
- 1 large green bell pepper, seeded and thinly sliced
- 1 large beefsteak tomato, thinly sliced
- 1 (4 oz) ball fresh mozzarella, thinly sliced
- ½ cup fresh basil leaves, roughly chopped

DIRECTIONS:

1. Preheat the oven to 425°F or 220°C.
2. Place a baking pan into the oven to heat.

To make the crust:

1. In a small mixing bowl, add the granulated sugar and hot water together, and mix until the sugar has dissolved. Add the instant yeast and whisk with a fork. Set aside.
2. In a medium-sized bowl, combine the flour, tapioca flour, and fine salt. Make a well in the center of the flour mixture and add the egg white and apple cider vinegar.
3. Pour the foamy yeast into the bowl with the flour and combine.
4. Add the potato starch and mix again.
5. Place the dough on a large sheet of parchment paper and spread it into a small circle with a spatula. It will be much wetter than traditional pizza dough.
6. Pour the canola oil onto the pizza dough and on your hands. Press the dough into a circle. Use your palms to press the center of the dough down and gently nudge the sides of the dough to be somewhat thicker. Allow this to rest for 10 minutes.
7. Place the pizza dough and parchment paper onto the preheated baking pan. Bake for 5 minutes.

To make the topping:

1. In a small mixing bowl, add the tomato sauce, chopped oregano and minced garlic, mix to combine, and set aside.
2. Meanwhile, melt the butter in a large, heavy-bottom pan over medium heat. Add the sliced mushrooms and fry for 5 minutes until browned.
3. Remove the pizza from the oven and cover it with the tomato sauce mixture, fried mushrooms, green bell pepper slices, sliced tomato, and sliced mozzarella cheese.
4. Return the pizza to the oven and bake for 8 to 10 minutes until the cheese has melted and gently browned.
5. Top with chopped fresh basil and serve.

ITALIAN SALAMI PIZZA

COOK TIME: 15 MIN | SERVES: 2–4

INGREDIENTS:

- Non-stick cooking spray
- 2 frozen cauliflower pizza crusts
- ½ cup canned tomato sauce
- 3 tbsp fresh basil, finely chopped and divided
- 1 tsp Italian seasoning
- ½ tsp garlic powder
- 2 cups shredded Colby Monterey Jack cheese, divided
- 7 oz Italian dried salami slices, divided

DIRECTIONS:

1. Preheat the oven to 425°F or 220°C. Coat 1 or 2 baking pans with non-stick cooking spray and place the pizza crusts on them.

2. In a small mixing bowl, add the tomato sauce, 1 tablespoon chopped basil, Italian seasoning and garlic powder, and mix to combine.

3. Spread 1/4 cup of the tomato sauce mixture in an even layer on top of each pizza crust.

4. Sprinkle 1 cup of shredded cheese, 1 tablespoon of basil, and half the Italian salami on the pizza crust. Repeat with the second pizza crust.

5. Bake for 12 to 15 minutes, or until the cheese has melted and the crust begins to turn golden brown.

6. Cool for 2 to 3 minutes before cutting into slices and serving.

VEGGIE EGG RICE

COOK TIME: 20 MIN | SERVES: 4

INGREDIENTS:

- 4 cups water
- 2 cups gluten-free, fluffy, white rice
- 2 tbsp sunflower oil
- 1 ½ cups frozen mixed vegetables, thawed
- 1 medium brown onion, diced
- 1 tbsp garlic, minced
- 4 spring onions, green parts chopped, plus extra for garnish
- 2 large eggs, beaten
- Fine salt
- Ground black pepper

DIRECTIONS:

1. In a large stockpot, bring the water to a boil. Add the white rice, stir, and cover. Cook for 10 to 15 minutes until the water is fully absorbed.

2. In a large, heavy-bottom pan, add the sunflower oil over medium heat until hot. Add the thawed mixed vegetables, diced onion, minced garlic and chopped spring onion, and cook for 3 minutes, stirring occasionally until the onions are lightly browned. Transfer the fried vegetable mixture into a medium mixing bowl.

3. In the same pan, add the eggs and cooked rice. Fry for 2 minutes, stirring often, or until the eggs are fully cooked.

4. Add the mixed vegetables into the pan with the rice mixture, season with fine salt and ground black pepper to taste, and mix to combine. Allow to fry for 1 to 2 minutes before removing from the heat and sprinkling with chopped spring onion. Serve warm.

ORANGE CHICKEN

COOK TIME: 1 HOUR | SERVES: 6

INGREDIENTS:

Marinade
- ½ cup gluten-free tamari
- ½ cup lemon juice
- 2 tsp garlic, minced
- 2 tsp ginger, grated
- 2 lb. chicken drumsticks
- Non-stick cooking spray

Drumstick Sauce
- ½ cup gluten-free orange marmalade
- ½ tsp fine salt
- ⅛ tsp garlic powder
- 1 tsp ginger, grated
- ⅛ tsp onion powder
- ¼ cup lemon juice

DIRECTIONS:

1. In a large, sealable plastic bag, add the tamari, lemon juice, minced garlic, grated ginger, and chicken drumsticks, seal, and turn the bag a few times to coat the drumsticks. Refrigerate overnight or for 2 hours, turning occasionally.

2. Preheat the oven to 375°F or 190°C.

3. Line a baking pan with aluminum foil. Coat a baking rack with non-stick cooking spray and place it into the pan. Place the drumsticks on the rack and bake for 15 minutes. Discard the leftover marinade.

4. In a medium-sized stockpot, add the orange marmalade, fine salt, garlic powder, grated ginger, onion powder and lemon juice, and whisk to combine. Cook for 2 minutes over medium heat and bring to a low boil.

5. Remove the drumsticks from the oven and baste with the orange marmalade sauce.

6. Bake for an additional 40 minutes, turning and basting the drumsticks every 10 minutes.

7. Take the drumsticks out of the oven and turn the oven to broil. Broil the chicken for 2–5 minutes until lightly charred. Serve warm.

CASHEW CHICKEN SKEWERS

COOK TIME: 5 MIN | SERVES: 4

INGREDIENTS:

Marinade
- 1 tbsp gluten-free tamari
- 3 tbsp lemon juice
- ¼ tsp fine salt
- ⅛ tsp ground black pepper
- 1 tbsp garlic, minced
- 1 tbsp ginger, grated
- ½ tsp ground coriander
- ½ tsp ground cumin
- ½ tsp ground turmeric
- 2 tbsp canola oil
- 2 lb. chicken breasts, skinless, boneless, and cut into cubes
- ¼ cup fresh parsley, chopped

Dipping Sauce
- 1 tsp ginger, grated
- ½ tsp garlic, minced
- ½ cup gluten-free cashew butter
- 2 tsp canola oil
- 2 tbsp gluten-free tamari
- 2 tbsp lemon juice
- 3 tbsp light brown sugar
- ½ tsp gluten-free sweet chili sauce
- ⅓ cup coconut milk

DIRECTIONS:

1. In a medium mixing bowl, add the tamari, lemon juice, fine salt, ground black pepper, minced garlic, grated ginger, ground coriander, ground cumin, ground turmeric and canola oil, and whisk to combine. Add the chicken and toss with the marinade, cover, and refrigerate for 30 minutes.

2. Preheat the grill. Skewer the marinated chicken cubes.

3. Grill the chicken for 4–5 minutes on each side until browned on both sides and cooked through. Sprinkle with chopped parsley.

4. In a small mixing bowl, add the grated ginger, minced garlic, cashew butter, canola oil, tamari, lemon juice, light brown sugar, sweet chili sauce, and coconut milk, whisk until smooth and serve on the side.

BBQ TOFU PATTIES

COOK TIME: 12 MIN | SERVES: 4

INGREDIENTS:

- 2 tbsp sunflower oil
- 1 (16 oz) super firm tofu block, halved horizontally and pressed
- 2 cups gluten-free sweet barbecue sauce
- 4 gluten-free Smartbun hamburger buns, halved
- 4 slices gluten-free cheese, ¼ inch thick
- 1 red onion, sliced into thin rings
- 4 butter lettuce leaves

DIRECTIONS:

1. In a large, heavy-bottom pan over medium heat, add the sunflower oil until hot.

2. Pat the tofu slices dry with paper towels and place them into the hot pan. Fry for 4 minutes on each side until a golden-brown crust is formed.

3. Place the fried tofu slices onto a cutting board and cut them into 6 slices. Return to the pan and reduce the heat to low.

4. Add the sweet barbecue sauce and fry the tofu in the sauce for 2 minutes until heated through. Set aside.

5. Preheat the broiler.

6. Place the cut hamburger buns under the broiler for 2 minutes, or until toasted.

7. Place a few slices of BBQ tofu with some sauce on the bottom half of each bun, top with sliced cheese, a few sliced onions, and 1 butter lettuce leaf. Serve immediately.

CRUMBLED TEMPEH BURGERS

COOK TIME: 15 MIN | SERVES: 4

INGREDIENTS:

- 3 tbsp sunflower oil
- 1 brown onion, finely chopped
- 1 tbsp garlic, minced
- Fine salt
- 2 (8oz) packages tempeh, crumbled
- 1 roasted green bell pepper, diced
- 1 (15 oz) can tomato sauce
- 3 tbsp light brown sugar
- 1 tbsp red wine vinegar
- 2 tbsp gluten-free Worcestershire sauce
- ½ tsp cayenne pepper
- Ground black pepper
- 4 gluten-free Smartbun hamburger buns, halved

DIRECTIONS:

1. Heat the sunflower oil in a large, heavy-bottom pan over medium heat until hot.

2. Add the chopped onion, minced garlic, and a pinch of salt. Fry for 5 minutes, stirring often until soft. Push the onion and garlic to the sides of the pan.

3. Add the crumbled tempeh to the pan and fry for 5 minutes until browned.

4. Add the roasted diced green pepper, tomato sauce, light brown sugar, red wine vinegar, Worcestershire sauce and cayenne pepper, and mix to combine.

5. Season with fine salt and ground black pepper to taste. Cook for an additional 5 minutes to allow the flavors to come together.

6. Top each hamburger roll with a generous scoop of the tempeh mixture and serve warm.

SHIITAKE CREAM RICE

COOK TIME: 45 MIN | SERVES: 6-8

INGREDIENTS:

- 3 tbsp unsalted butter
- 1 medium brown onion, diced
- 1 tbsp garlic, minced
- 1 tsp lime juice
- 1 tbsp parsley, chopped
- ½ cup dry white wine
- 2 cups risotto rice
- 1 ½ cups shiitake mushrooms, chopped
- 6 cups vegetable broth
- 1 cup parmesan cheese, shredded

DIRECTIONS:

1. Melt the butter in a large, heavy-bottom pan over medium heat. Add the minced garlic, lime juice and chopped parsley, and cook for 3 to 4 minutes, mixing often until fragrant.

2. Add the white wine and cook for 4 to 5 minutes mixing occasionally until the wine has reduced.

3. Add the risotto rice and mix to coat it well. Add the chopped shiitake mushrooms and incorporate. Add the vegetable broth ½ cup at a time, stirring constantly to avoid the rice sticking to the bottom.

4. Once all the broth has soaked into the rice, use a fork to check and, once tender, remove from the heat and serve immediately with a generous handful of shredded parmesan cheese. Serve warm.

Tip: if the rice is still undercooked, add more vegetable broth as needed until the rice is tender and all the liquid has been absorbed.

SIRLOIN MUSHROOM SAUCE

COOK TIME: 25 MIN | SERVES: 4

INGREDIENTS:

- 2 tbsp canola oil
- 1 tsp garlic, minced
- 8 oz whole, white mushrooms, sliced
- 4 sirloin steaks
- ¼ tsp onion powder
- ½ tsp ground black pepper
- 4 tbsp unsalted butter
- 4 tbsp Bob's Red Mill gluten-free 1-to-1 baking flour
- 1 cup beef broth
- 1 tbsp oregano, chopped
- 2 tbsp plain yogurt

DIRECTIONS:

1. Heat the oil in a large, heavy-bottom pan over medium heat until hot. Add the minced garlic and sliced mushrooms, and cook for 1 to 2 minutes, mixing occasionally until fragrant and golden brown.

2. Season each side of the sirloin steak with onion powder and ground black pepper. Place the steaks in the pan. Sear on each side for 3 to 6 minutes depending on the thickness, or until browned and cooked to your liking. Remove the steaks from the pan and set them aside to rest.

3. Reduce the heat to low and melt the butter into the mushrooms and garlic. Remove the pan off the heat and add the gluten-free flour and whisk until smooth.

4. Place the pan back on the heat and add the beef broth and chopped oregano. Increase the heat to medium and cook for 5 minutes, whisking constantly until smooth and the sauce has thickened.

5. Add the plain yogurt and whisk until it has melted into the sauce. Drizzle the mushroom sauce over the sirloin steak and serve.

Tip: you can use pork chops, chicken breasts or any other red meat in place of the sirloin.

THAI CHILI RICE

COOK TIME: 45 MIN | SERVES: 6

INGREDIENTS:

Rice
- 2 tbsp canola oil
- 2 cups jasmine rice, rinsed
- 2 ⅔ cups water

Stir-fry
- 2 brown onions, peeled and cut into quarters
- 5 red Thai chiles, stemmed
- 2 tbsp garlic, minced
- 3 tbsp light brown sugar
- 3 tbsp blackstrap molasses

- 3 tbsp gluten-free tamari
- 3 tbsp oyster sauce
- Fine salt
- 4 large eggs
- ½ cup canola oil
- 1 lb. cauliflower florets, cut into pieces
- 1 cup frozen peas, thawed
- ¼ cup water
- 1 small brown onion, sliced thinly

DIRECTIONS:

For the rice:

1. Heat a large stockpot over medium heat until hot, then add the canola oil and jasmine rice, and cook for 1 to 2 minutes. Pour the water and allow to boil. Reduce heat to low, cover, and let simmer for 16 to 18 minutes until rice is tender, and the water is absorbed.

2. Remove the pot from the heat, lay a clean, folded dish towel underneath the lid and let sit for 10 minutes. Transfer the cooked rice onto a rimmed baking sheet and spread it, allow to cool for 10 minutes, then refrigerate for 30 minutes.

For the stir-fry:

1. In a food processor, add the quartered onions, red Thai chiles, and garlic. Pulse the mixture into a coarse paste, and transfer into a bowl.

2. In a separate mixing bowl, add the light brown sugar, molasses, tamari, oyster sauce and fine salt, and mix to combine.

3. In another mixing bowl, add the eggs and fine salt to taste, and whisk to combine.

4. In a heavy-bottom pan, add the sliced onion and canola oil. Cook for 6 to 10 minutes over medium heat, stirring constantly until golden. Transfer the onions onto a paper, towel–lined plate and season with fine salt. Reserve the oil.

5. In the same pan over medium heat, add half of the whisked eggs and tilt the pan to coat the bottom. Cover and cook for 1½ minutes until the top is just set.

6. Slide the omelet onto a cutting board and roll it up into a tight log. Cut crosswise into 1-inch-wide segments; leave the segments rolled. Repeat with the remaining whisked egg.

7. In the same pan, add the cauliflower florets, thawed peas and water, and cover and cook over medium heat for 4 to 6 minutes until the cauliflower is tender, and the water is absorbed, then transfer to a small bowl. Remove rice from the refrigerator and break up any large clumps.

8. Heat the reserved oil in the same pan over medium heat until hot.

9. Add the chile mixture and cook for 3 to 5 minutes until golden. Add the molasses mixture and bring to a simmer.

10. Fold in rice and cauliflower and cook for 3 minutes, stirring constantly until heated through and evenly coated. Mix in the onions, transfer onto a platter and garnish the omelet rolls with fried shallots. Serve.

CRUMBED CHICKEN STRIPS

COOK TIME: 16 MIN | SERVES: 4

INGREDIENTS:

- 6 slices gluten-free sandwich bread, torn
- ½ tsp garlic powder
- ½ tsp Italian seasoning
- ½ tsp smoked paprika
- ½ cup cornstarch
- Fine salt
- Ground black pepper
- 2 large eggs
- 1 ½ lb. chicken breasts, boneless, skinless, and cut into wide strips
- ¾ cup canola oil

DIRECTIONS:

1. Preheat the oven to 425°F or 220°C.

2. Place the bread into a food processor, and process until it resembles breadcrumbs. Spread the crumbs in an even layer on a rimmed baking sheet and bake for 7 to 10 minutes, stirring occasionally until golden brown. Reduce oven temperature to 275°F or 140°C.

3. Transfer the breadcrumbs into a shallow dish, breaking up any large clumps into fine crumbs. Add in garlic powder, Italian seasoning, smoked paprika, 1 tablespoon cornstarch, ½ teaspoon fine salt, and 1/4 teaspoon ground black pepper, and mix to combine.

4. In another shallow dish, whisk the eggs. Place the remaining cornstarch in a large sealable bag.

5. Place a wire rack onto a rimmed baking sheet. Pat the chicken strips dry with paper towels and season with fine salt and ground black pepper.

6. Working in batches, place the chicken in the bag with the cornstarch, seal the bag, and shake to coat the chicken.

7. Use tongs to remove the chicken strips from the bag, shaking off excess cornstarch, dip in the eggs, then coat in the breadcrumb mixture, pressing gently to adhere. Place breaded chicken on the prepared wire rack.

8. Heat the canola oil in a large, heavy-bottom pan over medium heat until smoking. Add half of the crumbed chicken and cook for 4 to 6 minutes, flipping halfway until golden brown on all sides. Drain the chicken on paper towels, then transfer it onto a plate. Repeat with remaining breaded chicken. Serve.

CHILI CON CARNE

COOK TIME: 3-4 HOURS | SERVES: 6

INGREDIENTS:

- 2 tbsp canola oil
- 1 tsp garlic, minced
- 1 large red onion, peeled and diced
- 2 large green bell peppers, seeded and diced
- 1 lb. lean ground beef
- 1 (4oz) can diced green chili peppers
- 1 ¾ cups gluten-free beef broth
- 2 (15 oz) can red kidney beans, drained and rinsed
- 1 (15 oz) can butter beans, drained, and rinsed
- 1 (14 oz) can diced tomatoes, with their juices
- 2 (8 oz) cans tomato sauce
- 1 (6 oz) can tomato paste
- 1 tbsp ground coriander
- 2 tbsp cayenne pepper
- 2 tsp dried thyme
- 2 tbsp light brown sugar
- 1 tsp fine salt
- ¼ tsp ground black pepper

DIRECTIONS:

1. Heat the canola oil in a large, heavy bottom pan over medium heat until hot. Add the minced garlic, diced onions and diced green peppers, and sauté for 2 to 5 minutes until the vegetables have softened. Add the ground beef and cook for 5 to 8 minutes until no longer pink.

2. Add the ground beef mixture into a slow cooker. Add the diced green chilies, beef broth, kidney beans, butter beans, diced tomatoes with their juices, tomato sauce, tomato paste, ground coriander, cayenne pepper, dried thyme, light brown sugar, fine salt and ground black pepper, and mix to combine. Cover the slow cooker and allow to cook on high for 3 to 4 hours. Serve hot with your choice of side.

SOUPS & STEWS

CLAM SOUP

COOK TIME: 30 MIN | SERVES: 4

INGREDIENTS:

- 4 bacon slices, cut into strips
- 4 russet potatoes, peeled and diced
- 3 leeks, finely diced
- 1 brown onion, finely diced
- 1 tbsp garlic, minced
- 1 tsp parsley, finely chopped
- Fine salt
- 2 tbsp Bob's Red Mill gluten-free 1-to-1 baking flour
- 2 cups low-fat milk
- 2 cups low-sodium chicken broth
- Ground black pepper
- 2 (6 oz) cans clams, drained and roughly chopped

DIRECTIONS:

1. Add the bacon to a large stockpot over medium heat and cook for 8 minutes, stirring often until it renders most of its fat. Transfer the bacon onto a plate and set aside. Leave the bacon grease in the pot.

2. In the same pot, add the diced potatoes, diced leeks, diced onion, minced garlic and chopped parsley, and season with fine salt. Cook for 5 to 7 minutes, stirring often until the vegetables have softened.

3. Add the flour and cook for 2 minutes until thick and golden brown.

4. Pour in the low-fat milk and chicken broth, and allow to simmer. Season with fine salt and ground black pepper to taste. Cover and cook for 10 minutes until the vegetables are tender.

5. Add the chopped clams and cook for 1 minute until heated through.

6. Serve the clam soup in individual bowls and garnish with the cooked bacon.

TOMATO BEEF STEW

COOK TIME: 25 MIN | SERVES: 4

INGREDIENTS:

- 1 tbsp canola oil
- 1 lb. lean beef stew meat
- Sea salt
- Ground black pepper
- 4 red potatoes, peeled and quartered
- 4 carrots, unpeeled, scrubbed and cut into pieces
- 1 large brown onion, quartered lengthwise
- 2 tsp Italian seasoning
- 1 tbsp garlic, minced
- ½ cup dry red wine
- 1 (15 oz) can whole plum tomatoes, drained
- 2 cups gluten-free beef broth

DIRECTIONS:

1. In a large stockpot over medium heat, add the canola oil until hot.

2. Pat the stew meat dry with paper towels and generously season with fine salt and ground black pepper.

3. Add the seasoned meat into the pot and fry for 3 to 4 minutes. Add the quartered potatoes, carrots, quartered onion, Italian seasoning and minced garlic, and mix to combine.

4. Add the red wine and deglaze the pan by scraping up any browned bits from the bottom.

5. Add the drained tomatoes and beef broth. Cover and allow to simmer, reducing the heat to low. Cook for 20 minutes, or until the beef is cooked through and the potatoes are tender. Serve with your choice of side.

CHEESE & ONION SOUP

COOK TIME: 45 MIN | SERVES: 4

INGREDIENTS:

- 5 ⅓ tbsp unsalted butter
- 1 tbsp garlic, minced
- 3 tsp light brown sugar
- ½ tsp fine salt
- 3 medium brown onions, coarsely chopped
- 3 tbsp Bob's Red Mill gluten-free 1-to-1 baking flour
- 4 cups gluten-free beef broth
- 1 ½ tbsp gluten-free Worcestershire sauce
- 5 rosemary sprigs
- 1 cup gluten-free Swiss cheese, shredded

DIRECTIONS:

1. In a large stockpot over medium heat, add the butter, minced garlic, light brown sugar, fine salt and chopped onions, and mix to coat. Cook for 8 minutes until the onions have softened.

2. Preheat the oven to broil.

3. Add the flour and mix to coat the onions. Add the beef broth, 1 cup at a time, mixing between each cup until the mixture is smooth.

4. Add the Worcestershire sauce and rosemary sprigs. Allow the soup to simmer. Cook for 5 minutes, stirring occasionally, or until the soup starts to thicken. Remove the rosemary sprigs.

5. Divide the soup into oven-safe bowls, and sprinkle with shredded swiss cheese. Broil for 2 to 3 minutes, or until the cheese has melted and the edges are golden brown.

6. Allow to cool for 2 to 3 minutes before serving.

Tip: serve the cheese and onion soup with homemade gluten-free croutons or Aleia's Gluten-Free Classic Croutons.

THAI CHILI SOUP

COOK TIME: 20 MIN | SERVES: 4

INGREDIENTS:

- 2 tbsp coconut oil
- 1 tbsp garlic, minced
- ½ brown onion, finely chopped
- 2 tbsp gluten-free red Thai chili paste
- ¼ tsp ground ginger
- 4 cups vegetable broth
- 1 (13oz) can coconut milk
- 1 ½ tbsp oyster sauce
- 1 ½ tsp light brown sugar
- 8 oz gluten-free Thai rice noodles
- 2 cups fresh coriander, roughly chopped

DIRECTIONS:

1. In a large stockpot over medium heat, add the coconut oil until hot. Add the minced garlic and chopped onion, cook for 1 minute, then add the Thai chili paste and ground ginger, mix, and cook for 1 minute.

2. Add the vegetable broth, allow to simmer, and cook for 5 minutes. Add the coconut milk, oyster sauce, and light brown sugar, mix, and let it simmer for 3 minutes.

3. Add the Thai rice noodles and let it simmer for 4 minutes. Add the chopped coriander, mix, and let simmer for 2 minutes.

4. Remove off the heat and serve hot.

CHICKEN NOODLE SOUP

COOK TIME: 30 MIN | SERVES: 6

INGREDIENTS:

- 1 tbsp canola oil
- 3 large carrots, peeled and diced
- ½ brown onion, finely chopped
- 1 celery stalk, diced
- 1 tsp garlic, minced
- 2 tsp fresh parsley, finely chopped
- 5 cups gluten-free chicken broth
- ½ tsp fine salt
- ⅛ tsp ground black pepper
- 2 (5 oz) boneless, skinless chicken breasts, diced
- 1 cup gluten-free rice noodles, broken into bits

DIRECTIONS:

1. In a large stockpot over medium heat, add the canola oil until hot.

2. Add the diced carrots, chopped onion and diced celery, and fry for 5 to 7 minutes, stirring occasionally until tender.

3. Add the minced garlic, and chopped parsley, and fry for 30 seconds until fragrant.

4. Add the chicken broth, fine salt, and ground black pepper. Bring to a boil over medium heat.

5. Add the diced chicken and broken rice noodles, and mix to combine.

6. Allow the soup to simmer uncovered for 15 to 20 minutes, or until the noodles are cooked. Remove from the heat, cover and let it sit for 5 minutes. Serve warm.

BEEF BEAN SOUP

COOK TIME: 4 HOURS | SERVES: 6

INGREDIENTS:

- 1 tbsp canola oil
- 2 (14 oz) cans diced tomatoes, with their juices
- 1 tbsp garlic powder
- 1 tbsp onion powder
- 1 tbsp Italian seasoning
- 2 gluten-free beef cubes
- 1 (16 oz) can kidney beans, drained and rinsed
- 1 (16 oz) can butter beans, drained, and rinsed
- 1 (16 oz) can pinto beans, drained and rinsed
- 2 medium carrots, peeled and chopped
- 1 cup green beans, trimmed and chopped
- 1 large courgette, diced
- 1 medium butternut squash, seeds removed and diced
- 1 (10 oz) package baby spinach
- 1 lb. lean beef stew meat
- 1 cup water
- Extra fine salt
- Ground black pepper

DIRECTIONS:

1. Add the canola oil to the bottom of a slow cooker.

2. Add the diced tomatoes with their juices, garlic powder, onion powder, Italian seasoning, beef cubes, drained kidney beans, butter beans, pinto beans, chopped carrots, trimmed green beans, diced courgette, diced butternut squash, baby spinach, and beef stew meat, and mix to combine.

3. Add the water and season with fine salt and ground black pepper to taste.

4. Cook on high for 4 hours, or until the vegetables have softened. Season with extra fine salt and ground black pepper if desired. Serve hot.

Tip: if the soup is too thick, you can thin it out by adding 1/4 cup hot water at a time until it has reached the consistency you prefer.

POTATO TURKEY SOUP

COOK TIME: 25 MIN | SERVES: 4

INGREDIENTS:

- 1 tbsp sunflower oil
- 1 brown onion, diced
- 1 tbsp garlic, minced
- 4 cups chicken broth
- 2 cups sweet potatoes, peeled and diced
- 1 green bell pepper, cut into thin strips
- 1 (14 oz) can corn kernels, drained, and rinsed
- 1 cup salsa verde
- 1 tsp ground coriander
- 1 tsp smoked paprika
- Pinch cayenne pepper
- 2 boneless skinless turkey breasts, cut into cubes
- Fine salt
- Ground black pepper
- 1 tsp lemon juice
- 8 oz sour cream
- ½ cup fresh parsley, roughly chopped

DIRECTIONS:

1. In a large stockpot over medium heat, add the sunflower oil until hot.

2. Add the diced onion and minced garlic, fry for 5 minutes, stirring often, until soft.

3. Add the chicken broth, diced sweet potatoes, green bell pepper, rinsed corn, salsa verde, ground coriander, smoked paprika, cayenne pepper, and cubed turkey breasts. Season with fine salt and ground pepper to taste, and mix to combine.

4. Allow to simmer, cover, and cook for 20 minutes until the sweet potatoes are tender and the turkey is cooked through. Add the lemon juice and mix.

5. Ladle the soup into serving bowls and drizzle with sour cream and chopped parsley. Serve hot.

MIXED VEGETABLE SOUP

COOK TIME: 20 MIN | SERVES: 4-6

INGREDIENTS:

- ½ cup olive oil, divided
- 2 tbsp garlic, minced
- 2 medium carrots, peeled and diced
- 2 celery stalks, diced
- 1 brown onion, diced
- 1 (28 oz) can plum tomatoes, crushed
- 3 small red potatoes, peeled and diced
- ½ fennel bulb, cored and diced
- 1 (15 oz) can butter beans, rinsed and drained
- 4 cups vegetable broth
- Fine salt
- Ground black pepper
- 8 oz gluten-free chickpea shell pasta
- 2 tbsp cilantro, roughly chopped
- ¼ cup basil leaves, roughly chopped
- 2 oz parmesan cheese, shredded

DIRECTIONS:

1. In a large stockpot over medium heat, add 2 tablespoons of olive oil until hot.

2. Add the minced garlic, diced carrots, diced celery, and diced onion, and fry for 5 minutes, stirring occasionally until fragrant and beginning to soften.

3. Add the crushed tomatoes, diced potatoes, diced fennel, butter beans, and vegetable broth. Season with fine salt and ground black pepper to taste. Allow to simmer for 5 minutes, stirring occasionally.

4. Add the pasta shells, chopped cilantro, and chopped basil. Cook for 10 minutes, stirring occasionally until the pasta is al dente.

5. Ladle the soup into serving bowls, drizzle each bowl with 1 tablespoon of the remaining olive oil, and top with shredded parmesan cheese. Serve hot.

MEXICAN STEW

COOK TIME: 20 MIN | SERVES: 6-8

INGREDIENTS:

- 2 tbsp canola oil
- 1 tbsp garlic, minced
- ½ red onion, chopped
- 1 lb. ground beef
- 2/3 cup cornstarch
- 2 ½ cups gluten-free beef broth
- 3 (10 oz) cans diced tomatoes
- 2 tbsp diced green chiles
- 1 (10 oz) can gluten-free red enchilada sauce
- ¾ tsp ground coriander
- Fine salt
- Ground black pepper
- 2 cups cheddar cheese, shredded
- Pico de gallo, for garnish

DIRECTIONS:

1. In a large stockpot over medium heat, add the canola oil until hot. Add the minced garlic and chopped onion, and cook for 5 minutes until the onion is translucent. Add the ground beef, breaking it up with a fork, and cook for 5 to 7 minutes, stirring occasionally until completely browned.

2. Add the cornstarch and cook for 1 minute, or until all the liquid has been absorbed.

3. Immediately add the beef broth, diced tomatoes, enchilada sauce, ground coriander, fine salt and ground black pepper to taste, and mix to combine.

4. Allow to simmer, and cook for 5 minutes, stirring occasionally, or until the liquid has reduced.

5. Remove from the heat, add the grated cheddar cheese, and mix until melted and blended. Top with pico de gallo and serve warm.

CHEESE & BACON SOUP

COOK TIME: 52 MIN | SERVES: 6

INGREDIENTS:

- 3 tbsp unsalted butter
- ½ large brown onion, chopped
- 2 tsp garlic, minced
- 4 large russet potatoes, peeled and cubed
- 3 cups gluten-free chicken broth
- 1 ½ tsp garlic powder
- 1 tsp fine salt
- 1 tsp ground black pepper
- 1 cup whole milk
- 1 ½ cups cheddar cheese, divided
- 8 tbsp spring onions, chopped and divided
- 8 tbsp bacon crumbles, divided

DIRECTIONS:

1. Melt the unsalted butter in a large stockpot over medium heat. Add the chopped onion and minced garlic and cook for 2 minutes, stirring occasionally until fragrant.

2. Add the potato cubes, chicken broth, garlic powder, fine salt, and ground black pepper. Mix and allow to simmer for 4 minutes.

3. Use an immersion blender to mash the potatoes. Add the whole milk, 1 cup shredded cheddar cheese, 4 tablespoons chopped spring onion, and 4 tablespoons bacon crumbles, and mix to incorporate. Cook for 8 minutes, or until the cheese has melted.

4. Divide into serving bowls and top with the remaining cheese, chopped spring onion, and bacon crumbles. Serve warm.

TOMATO & BASIL SOUP

COOK TIME: 40 MIN | SERVES: 6

INGREDIENTS:

- 4 tbsp coconut oil
- ½ large brown onion, peeled and sliced
- 1 ½ cups gluten-free vegetable stock
- 1 (28 oz) can peeled tomatoes, with their juices
- ½ tsp fine salt
- 1 tsp granulated sugar
- ¼ cup fresh basil, roughly chopped

DIRECTIONS:

1. Add the coconut oil to a large stockpot over medium heat. Add the sliced onions, vegetable stock, peeled tomatoes with their juices, fine salt and granulated sugar, and mix to combine.

2. Allow to simmer uncovered and cook for 40 minutes stirring occasionally.

3. Blend with an immersion blender until smooth and well combined. Ladle into serving bowls and garnish with chopped basil. Serve warm.

CHINESE EGGS SOUP

COOK TIME: 10 MIN | SERVES: 4

INGREDIENTS:

- 2 tsp sesame oil
- 1 tbsp ginger, grated
- 1 tbsp garlic, minced
- ½ cup shitake mushrooms, sliced
- 3 tbsp gluten-free tamari
- 1 tbsp rice wine vinegar
- 6 cups gluten-free chicken stock
- 4 servings gluten-free rice ramen noodles
- 2 large soft-boiled eggs, halved
- ¼ cup spring onion, sliced
- 4 tbsp sesame seeds, toasted

DIRECTIONS:

1. Heat the sesame oil in a large stockpot over medium heat. Add the grated ginger and minced garlic and fry for 30 seconds until fragrant.

2. Add the sliced mushrooms and fry for 2 minutes until tender. Add the tamari and rice wine vinegar, and mix to combine.

3. Add the chicken stock, cover, and bring to a boil. Remove the lid and let simmer uncovered for 2 minutes.

4. Add the rice noodles to the pot and cook for 5 minutes or until the ramen is fully cooked.

5. Divide the noodles into four bowls, ladle in the broth, and top with half of a soft-boiled egg, sliced spring onions and toasted sesame seeds. Serve hot.

CHICKEN STEW

COOK TIME: 2 HOURS 10 MIN | SERVES: 4

INGREDIENTS:

- 1 ½ lb. chicken breasts, cubed
- ¼ cup Bob's Red Mill gluten-free 1-to-1 baking flour
- 3 tbsp canola oil
- 1 medium brown onion, roughly chopped
- Fine salt
- Ground black pepper
- 3 cups gluten-free chicken broth
- 1 (6 oz) can tomato paste
- 1 tbsp garlic, minced
- 4 tbsp gluten-free Worcestershire sauce
- 2 ½ tsp basil leaves, chopped
- 1 ½ tbsp Italian seasoning
- 5 red potatoes, peeled and cut into cubes
- 2 cups frozen peas and carrots

DIRECTIONS:

1. Place the chicken cubes in a large resealable bag, add the flour, seal, and shake until the chicken is coated in flour.

2. In a Dutch oven over medium heat, add the canola oil until hot. Add the chopped onions and cook for 2 to 3 minutes until fragrant and golden.

3. Add the cut chicken and cook for 5 minutes until browned. Season with fine salt and ground black pepper to taste.

4. Add the chicken broth, tomato paste, minced garlic, Worcestershire sauce, chopped basil, and Italian seasoning. Mix to combine and allow to boil. Reduce the heat to low and simmer, uncovered, for 1 hour.

5. Add the cut potatoes and frozen peas and carrots, cover, and cook for an additional 1 hour. Serve warm with your choice of side.

MEAT, POULTRY, & SEAFOOD

CRISPY CHICKEN

COOK TIME: 50 MIN | SERVES: 6

INGREDIENTS:

- Non-stick cooking spray
- 1 tbsp light brown sugar, packed
- 1 tbsp garlic powder
- 1 tbsp onion powder
- 1 tbsp fine salt
- 2 tbsp smoked paprika
- ½ tsp cayenne pepper
- 1 tbsp ground cumin
- 1 tsp ground coriander
- 1 tsp mustard powder
- 6 (4 oz) boneless, skinless chicken breasts
- ¾ cup gluten-free breadcrumbs
- ½ cup dairy-free buttery spread, melted

DIRECTIONS:

1. Preheat the oven to 375°F or 190°C. Coat a baking dish with nonstick cooking spray. Place chicken breasts in the baking dish.

2. In a small mixing bowl, add the light brown sugar, garlic powder, onion powder, fine salt, smoked paprika, cayenne pepper, ground cumin, ground coriander and mustard powder, and whisk to combine.

3. Rub 1 tablespoon of the seasoning mixture on each chicken breast.

4. Generously sprinkle breadcrumbs over the chicken breasts and press to down to stick.

5. Drizzle the melted buttery spread over the chicken.

6. Bake for 50 minutes, or until the chicken is no longer pink. Serve with your choice of side.

LAMB CREAM CURRY

COOK TIME: 1 HOUR 36 MIN | SERVES: 4

INGREDIENTS:

- 1 tbsp canola oil
- 1 lb. lamb stew meat
- 1 (13 oz) can unsweetened coconut cream
- 2 tbsp honey
- 1 tsp ground cinnamon
- 1 tsp ground turmeric
- ½ tsp ground ginger
- ¼ tsp fine salt
- ½ cup golden raisins
- 2 large russet potatoes, cut into cubes
- ½ cup frozen peas, thawed
- ½ cup fresh coriander, chopped

DIRECTIONS:

1. Heat the canola oil in a large stockpot over medium heat. Fry the lamb meat for 5 to 6 minutes until browned.

2. Add the coconut cream and honey, and mix to coat the lamb. Add the ground cinnamon, ground turmeric, ground ginger, fine salt, and golden raisins, and mix to combine.

3. Reduce the heat to low, cover, and allow to simmer for 1 hour, stirring occasionally until sauce thickens.

4. Add the thawed peas, chopped coriander, and allow to simmer for an additional 30 minutes, stirring occasionally. Serve hot with rice or gluten-free naan bread.

MAHI MAHI TORTILLAS

COOK TIME: 8 MIN | SERVES: 4

INGREDIENTS:

- 3 tbsp canola oil
- 1 lemon, zested and juiced
- 1 tsp ground coriander
- 1 tsp red pepper flakes
- ¼ tsp fine salt
- ½ tsp smoked paprika
- 1 lb. mahi mahi, cut into strips
- ½ cup lite mayonnaise
- ½ cup sour cream
- ¼ cup fresh parsley, chopped
- 16 gluten-free corn tortillas
- 1 cup green cabbage, julienned
- ½ medium red onion, thinly sliced
- 1 cup pico de gallo

DIRECTIONS:

1. In a large mixing bowl, add the 2 tablespoons canola oil, lemon zest, lemon juice, ground coriander, red pepper flakes, fine salt, and smoked paprika, and mix to combine. Add the mahi mahi strips, toss to coat, and refrigerate for 15 minutes.

2. In a small measuring jug, add the lite mayonnaise, sour cream, and chopped parsley, whisk to combine, and refrigerate until ready to serve.

3. Heat the 1 tablespoon canola oil in a large heavy bottom pan over medium heat until hot. Remove the mahi mahi from the marinade, add to the pan, and fry for 3 to 4 minutes on each side, or until it flakes easily with a fork.

4. Divide the cooked fish among the corn tortillas. Top each tortilla with some of the shredded cabbage, sliced onion, and pico de gallo. Finish with a tablespoon of the mayonnaise and parsley sauce.

LIME SHRIMP SKEWERS

COOK TIME: 10 MIN | SERVES: 4

INGREDIENTS:

- 2 tbsp garlic, minced
- 1 tbsp smoked paprika
- ¼ tsp red pepper flakes
- ½ tsp fine salt
- ⅛ tsp cayenne pepper
- 2 tbsp sunflower oil
- 2 limes, zested and juiced
- 2 lb. jumbo shrimp, peeled and deveined
- 2 medium courgettes, halved lengthwise and cut into bite-size cubes
- 16 oz grape tomatoes
- 1 medium red onion, cut into bite-size cubes

DIRECTIONS:

1. In a small mixing bowl, add the minced garlic, smoked paprika, red pepper flakes, fine salt, cayenne pepper, sunflower oil, lime zest, and lime juice, whist to combine.

2. Alternating between the shrimp and vegetables, thread them onto bamboo or wooden skewers and place them in a shallow dish.

3. Pour the lime marinade over the skewers and allow to marinade for 10 minutes.

4. Heat a grill pan on medium heat for 5 minutes until hot. Sear the skewers for 3 to 4 minutes on each side, continuously basting with the marinade until the vegetables are lightly charred, and the shrimp is fully cooked. Serve immediately.

CITRUS FRIED CHICKEN

COOK TIME: 10 MIN | SERVES: 4

INGREDIENTS:

- ¾ cup chicken broth
- 1 ½ tsp orange zest plus 8 strips zest
- ¾ cup orange juice
- 1 ½ tsp lemon zest plus 8 strips zest
- 4 tbsp lemon juice
- 1 ½ tsp lime zest plus 8 strips zest
- 4 tbsp lime juice
- 6 tbsp distilled white vinegar
- ½ cup light brown sugar
- ¼ cup gluten-free tamari

- 1 tbsp garlic, minced
- 1 tbsp ginger, grated
- ½ tsp cayenne pepper
- 1 ½ lb. boneless, skinless chicken thighs, trimmed and cut into pieces
- 2 tbsp water
- 5 tsp plus 1 cup cornstarch
- 3 large egg whites
- ½ tsp baking soda
- 3 cups canola oil

DIRECTIONS:

1. In a medium-sized stockpot, add the chicken broth, orange zest, orange juice, lemon zest, lemon juice, lime zest, lime juice, white vinegar, light brown sugar, tamari, minced garlic, grated ginger, and 1/4 teaspoon cayenne pepper, whisk until the sugar has dissolved. Do not heat it.

2. Pour a ¾ cup of the liquid mixture into a large sealable bag, add the chicken pieces, and toss to coat, pressing out as much air as possible and seal the bag. Refrigerate chicken for 30 minutes or up to 1 hour. Bring the remaining mixture in the pot to a boil over high heat.

3. In a small bowl, add the water and 5 teaspoons cornstarch, mix, and then whisk into the pot and cook for 1 minute until the mixture has thickened. Turn off the heat, and add the orange, lemon, and lime zest strips, cover and set aside.

4. In a shallow dish, beat egg whites until frothy. In a large sealable bag, add the remaining 1 cup cornstarch, baking soda and the remaining 1/4 teaspoon cayenne pepper, and mix to combine.

5. Pat the chicken pieces dry with paper towels. Working in batches, coat the chicken in egg whites, then place it in the bag with the cornstarch, and shake to coat. Shake off excess cornstarch and place them on a plate.

6. Heat the canola oil in large Dutch oven over medium heat until hot. Add half of the chicken pieces to the hot oil and fry for 5 minutes until golden brown, turning chicken as needed.

7. Transfer the chicken onto paper, towel–lined wire rack. Repeat with the remaining chicken.

8. Reheat the citrus sauce over medium heat for 2 minutes until simmering. Add the fried chicken and toss to coat and heat through. Serve warm.

ONE-POT PATTIES

COOK TIME: 30 MIN | SERVES: 6

INGREDIENTS:

- 1 lb. lean ground beef
- ½ medium green bell pepper, seeds removed and diced
- ½ medium red bell pepper, seeds removed and diced
- ½ cup gluten-free breadcrumbs
- 1 large egg
- 3 ½ tsp tomato sauce, divided
- 2 tsp gluten free Worcestershire sauce, divided
- 1 tsp onion powder, divided
- 1 tsp garlic powder, divided
- ¼ tsp fine salt
- 1 tsp olive oil
- 2 tbsp Bob's Red Mill gluten-free 1-to-1 baking flour
- 1 ½ cups gluten-free beef broth
- 1 cup shiitake mushrooms, chopped

DIRECTIONS:

1. In a large mixing bowl, add the ground beef, diced green bell pepper, diced red bell pepper, breadcrumbs, egg, 2 teaspoons of tomato sauce, 1 teaspoon of Worcestershire sauce, ½ teaspoon of onion powder, ½ teaspoon garlic powder and fine salt. Mix well.

2. In a large heavy bottom pan, heat the olive oil over medium heat.

3. Form the beef mixture into 9 patties. Working in batches, place them in the hot pan and cook for 4 minutes on each side. Transfer the patties onto a plate and repeat with the remaining patties. Reserve the juices in the pan.

4. In a small mixing bowl, add the remaining 1½ teaspoons of tomato sauce, remaining 1 teaspoon of Worcestershire sauce, remaining ½ teaspoon of onion powder, ½ teaspoon garlic powder and the flour, and mix to combine.

5. Add the flour mixture into the pan with the reserved juices, and cook, stirring for 1 minute. Add the beef broth and chopped mushrooms, mix, and bring to a simmer. Cook for 5 to 7 minutes until the liquid start to thicken.

6. Return the beef patties to the pan and cook for 1 minute, or until fully cooked. Remove from the heat and serve immediately.

CHICKEN TORTILLA ROLLS

COOK TIME: 35 MIN | SERVES: 4-6

INGREDIENTS:

- ¼ cup canola oil
- 1 medium onion, chopped fine
- 3 tbsp chili powder
- 1 tbsp garlic, minced
- 3 tsp ground coriander
- 3 tsp ground cumin
- 2 tsp light brown sugar
- ½ tsp fine salt
- 1 lb. boneless, skinless chicken breasts, trimmed and cut into strips
- 2 (8 oz) cans tomato sauce
- 1 cup water
- ½ cup fresh parsley, chopped
- ¼ cup jarred jalapeños, chopped
- 3 cups cheddar cheese, shredded
- 12 gluten-free corn tortillas

DIRECTIONS:

1. Heat 2 tablespoons of canola oil in a medium stockpot over medium heat until hot. Add the chopped onion and cook for 5 to 7 minutes until softened. Add the chili powder, minced garlic, ground coriander, ground cumin, light brown sugar, and fine salt and cook for 30 seconds until fragrant.

2. Add the chicken strips and coat thoroughly with spices. Add the tomato sauce and water, allow to simmer, and cook for 8 minutes, or until the chicken is cooked through.

3. Strain the mixture through a fine-mesh strainer set over a bowl, pressing on the chicken mixture to extract as much liquid as possible. Transfer the chicken mixture into a separate bowl, and refrigerate for 10 minutes. Add the chopped parsley, jarred jalapeños, and 2½ cups cheddar cheese, and mix to combine.

4. Preheat the oven to 450°F or 230°C.

5. Spread ¾ cup of the sauce over the bottom of a deep baking dish. Brush both sides of the corn tortillas with the remaining 2 tablespoons canola oil.

6. Stack the tortillas, wrap them in a damp dish towel, and place them on a plate. Microwave for 1 minute until warm and pliable.

7. Working with 1 warm tortilla at a time, spread 1/3 cup of the chicken filling across the center of the tortilla. Roll the tortilla tightly around the filling and place it seam side down in the baking dish. Arrange the tortillas in 2 columns across the width of the dish.

8. Pour the remaining sauce over top of the tortillas to cover completely, and sprinkle the remaining ½ cup shredded cheddar cheese down the center of each tortilla.

9. Cover the dish tightly with greased aluminum foil. Bake for 15 to 20 minutes, or until the tortillas are heated through and the cheese has melted. Serve warm.

BBQ DRUMSTICKS

COOK TIME: 50 MIN | SERVES: 4-6

INGREDIENTS:

- ½ cup ketchup
- ¼ cup gluten-free tamari
- ¼ cup gluten-free Worcestershire sauce
- ½ cup light brown sugar
- 4 tbsp canola oil
- 1 tsp red pepper flakes
- 2 tbsp Smokey Mesquite seasoning or any of choice
- 4 lb. chicken drumsticks

DIRECTIONS:

1. Preheat the oven to 275°F or 140°C. Line a rimmed baking pan with aluminum foil and set a wire rack in it.

2. In a medium-sized measuring jug, add the ketchup, tamari, Worcestershire sauce, light brown sugar, canola oil, red pepper flakes and seasoning, and whisk to combine.

3. Dry the drumsticks with paper towels and place them into a large bowl. Arrange the drumsticks, in a single layer on the prepared wire rack.

4. Roast the drumsticks for 30 minutes. Remove from the oven and increase the oven temperature to 425°F or 220°C.

5. Bake for 40 to 50 minutes, basting the drumsticks every 10 minutes.

6. Remove the sticky drumsticks from the oven and let them stand for 5 minutes before serving.

Tip: if you want more sauce on your drumsticks, add the left-over BBQ marinade into a stockpot and cook for 5 minutes or until bubbling, then pour it into a large bowl. Add the fully cooked drumsticks into the marinade and toss to coat.

LIME & MAPLE SALMON

COOK TIME: 10 MIN | SERVES: 4

INGREDIENTS:

- 1 cup gluten-free tamari
- ¼ cup maple syrup
- 3 tbsp lime juice
- 1 lime, zested
- 1 tbsp ginger, grated
- 1 tbsp garlic, minced
- 4 (4 oz) salmon fillets

DIRECTIONS:

1. In a large mixing bowl, add the tamari, maple syrup, lime juice, lime zest, grated ginger, and minced garlic, and whisk until the maple syrup has dissolved.

2. Place the salmon fillets in the lime marinade skin-side up. Cover the bowl with plastic wrap and marinate for 20 minutes in the refrigerator.

3. Preheat the broiler to high. Put the marinated salmon on an aluminum, foil-lined baking pan, and coat with nonstick cooking spray.

4. Place the salmon under the broiler skin-side down and broil for 7 to 10 minutes until the fish is well caramelized and is cooked through. Serve with your choice of side.

CITRUS FRIED MUSSELS

COOK TIME: 8 MIN | SERVES: 4

INGREDIENTS:

- 2 tbsp canola oil
- 2 lb. fully cooked mussels
- ½ tsp fine salt
- ¼ tsp ground black pepper
- 4 tbsp unsalted butter, divided
- 2 tsp garlic, minced
- ¼ cup white cooking wine
- 2 tbsp lime juice
- 2 tbsp lemon juice
- 2 tbsp orange juice
- ¼ cup fresh cilantro, chopped

DIRECTIONS:

1. Heat canola oil in a large heavy bottom pan over medium heat. Remove the mussels from the shell if needed and season with fine salt and ground black pepper. Add the mussels to the pan and fry for 2 minutes. Remove from the pan and set aside.

2. Melt 2 tablespoons of butter in the pan. Add the garlic and cook for 2 minutes until fragrant. Pour in white cooking wine and bring to a simmer for 2 minutes until the wine has reduced by half. Mix in the remaining tablespoon of butter and add the lime juice, lemon juice and orange juice, and allow to simmer for 3 minutes.

3. Remove the pan from the heat and add the mussels back into the pan to warm up. Garnish with chopped cilantro and serve with your choice of side.

Tip: if you want to thicken the sauce, mix 1 teaspoon of cornstarch with 2 tablespoons of water, and added it to the liquid mixture in step 2 with the citrus juices.

MERLOT WINE STEAK

COOK TIME: 20 MIN | SERVES: 4

INGREDIENTS:

- 2 tbsp canola, divided
- 4 sirloin steaks
- Fine salt
- Ground black pepper
- 2 medium courgettes, quartered lengthwise, cut into pieces
- ½ cup Merlot wine

DIRECTIONS:

1. Heat 1 tablespoon of canola oil in a large, heavy-bottom pan over medium heat until hot.

2. Pat the steaks dry with paper towels and season both sides with fine salt and ground black pepper. Place the steaks in the pan and cook for 5 minutes until well browned. Flip and cook for 4 to 5 minutes, or until cooked through. Transfer onto serving plates.

3. Add 1 tablespoon of canola oil into a now-empty pan.

4. Add the courgette pieces and fry for 4 minutes until browned on the outside but still firm. Season with fine salt and ground black pepper, and transfer onto the serving plates.

5. Pour the Merlot wine into the pan. Allow it to simmer for 2 minutes, stirring often until reduced.

6. Pour the merlot sauce over the steaks and courgettes and serve warm.

LOBSTER RICE BOWL

COOK TIME: 45 MIN | SERVES: 4

INGREDIENTS:

- 1 ½ cups white rice
- 2 cups water
- Fine salt
- 1 tsp ginger, grated
- 1 tsp garlic, minced
- 2 tbsp gluten-free tamari, plus more for serving
- 1 tbsp sweet chili sauce
- 1 tbsp plus 1 tsp sesame oil, divided
- 1 tbsp lemon juice
- 1 tbsp honey
- 2 (7 oz) packet lobster tails, peeled, deveined, and roughly chopped
- 4 cups baby spinach
- 1 cup shiitake mushrooms, chopped
- 1 tbsp sunflower oil
- 4 large eggs

DIRECTIONS:

1. In a medium stockpot over high heat, bring the rice, water, and a generous pinch salt to a boil. Cover and cook on high for 20 minutes, or until the rice is cooked.

2. In a small mixing bowl, add the ginger, minced garlic, tamari, sweet chili sauce, 1 tablespoon of the sesame oil, lemon juice, and honey, and whisk to combine. Allow it to rest for 5 minutes.

3. In a large, heavy-bottom pan over medium heat, fry the chopped lobster meat and the sauce for 10 minutes until cooked through and opaque. Transfer to a clean bowl.

4. In the same pan over medium heat. Add the remaining 1 teaspoon sesame oil, baby spinach, and chopped mushrooms. Fry for 3 to 5 minutes, or until the spinach is soft and most of the moisture has evaporated. Transfer to a clean bowl.

5. In another frying pan placed over high heat. Add the sunflower oil and tilt the pan to coat the bottom. Carefully crack the eggs into the pan and fry for 3 to 5 minutes until set.

6. Divide the cooked rice among 4 serving bowls. Top each bowl of rice with cooked lobster and spinach, and top with a fried egg. Serve warm with a drizzle of tamari.

Substitution tip: you can replace the lobster meat with shrimp meat in this recipe.

CRUMBED BRIE CHICKEN

COOK TIME: 45 MIN | SERVES: 4

INGREDIENTS:

- Non-stick cooking spray
- 2 large eggs
- 1½ cups gluten-free panko breadcrumbs
- ½ tsp garlic powder
- ¼ tsp onion powder
- ¼ tsp smoked paprika
- 4 chicken breasts, butterflied vertically
- 4 slices ham
- 4 slices brie cheese
- Chopped fresh cilantro, for garnish

DIRECTIONS:

1. Preheat the oven to 350°F or 180°C. Coat a deep baking dish with non-stick cooking spray.

2. In a medium mixing bowl, beat the eggs lightly with a fork. In another mixing bowl, add the breadcrumbs, garlic powder, onion powder, and smoked paprika, and mix to combine.

3. Dip the chicken breasts into the beaten egg, allowing the excess to drip off. Place the chicken into the breadcrumb mixture, making sure each piece is coated well.

4. Fold the coated chicken breasts back into their original shape and place them into the baking dish. Bake for 15 minutes until the breadcrumbs turn a darker golden brown along the edges.

5. Carefully open each breast enough to place one slice of ham and one slice of brie cheese. Press the chicken closed.

6. Bake the chicken breasts for an additional 30 to 35 minutes or until cooked through. Serve hot and garnished with chopped cilantro.

SWEET & SOUR BEEF

COOK TIME: 55 MIN | SERVES: 4

INGREDIENTS:

- ⅓ cup canola oil
- 2 large eggs
- 1½ cups cornstarch
- 1 tbsp plus 1½ tsp garlic powder, divided
- ¼ tsp fine salt
- ¼ tsp ground black pepper
- 1 ½ cups white rice flour
- 1 ½ lb. lean beef stew meat
- 7 tbsp gluten-free sweet chili sauce
- 1 cup granulated sugar
- ⅓ cup apple cider vinegar
- 4 tbsp gluten-free tamari

DIRECTIONS:

1. Preheat the oven to 350°F or 180°C. Coat the bottom of a baking dish with canola oil.

2. In a medium mixing bowl, beat the eggs lightly with a fork.

3. In a large resealable bag, add the cornstarch, 1 tablespoon garlic powder, fine salt and ground black pepper, and shake to mix. In another large sealable bag, add the white rice flour.

4. Working in batches, dip the beef pieces into the beaten eggs, allowing excess egg to drip off. Then place the beef pieces into the bag with the rice flour, seal tightly, and shake until evenly coated. Transfer the coated beef into the bag with the cornstarch mixture and repeat the shaking technique.

5. Place the coated beef pieces into the baking dish and bake for 40 minutes, stirring every 15 minutes to allow the beef to cook and crisp up evenly.

6. In a medium-sized bowl, add the sweet chili sauce, granulated sugar, apple cider vinegar, tamari and the remaining 1½ teaspoons of garlic powder, and mix to combine. Remove the beef from the oven and pour the sauce over the top, mix to coat.

7. Return to the oven and bake for an additional 10 minutes, or until the beef is fully cooked and the sauce starts to thicken. Remove from the oven and let the beef cool for 5 minutes before serving. The sauce will continue to thicken while cooling.

SIDES & SAUCES

LIME ROASTED VEG

COOK TIME: 25 MIN | SERVES: 4

INGREDIENTS:

- 4 large carrots, peeled, halved lengthwise and cut into pieces
- 1 small yellow onion, cut into wedges
- 1 courgette, halved lengthwise and cut into pieces
- 2 yellow potatoes, quartered
- 6 tbsp canola oil, divided
- Fine salt
- Ground black pepper
- 1 cup basil leaves
- 1 lime, zested
- 1 lime, juiced
- ½ tbsp garlic, minced

DIRECTIONS:

1. Preheat the oven to 425°F or 220°C.

2. On a rimmed baking pan, add the carrot pieces, onion wedges, courgette pieces, and quartered potatoes, spread the vegetables evenly on the pan. Drizzle with 1½ tablespoons of the canola oil and season with fine salt and ground black pepper, toss to coat.

3. Roast, uncovered, for 20 to 25 minutes until the vegetables are tender.

4. In a blender, add the remaining 4½ tablespoons canola oil, basil leaves, lime zest, lime juice and minced garlic, and blend until smooth. Season with fine salt.

5. Transfer the roasted vegetables onto a serving platter and pour the lime and basil oil over them. Serve warm

CRUMBED TOMATOES

COOK TIME: 10 MIN | SERVES: 6

INGREDIENTS:

- 1 large green tomato, cut into thick slices
- Fine salt
- Ground black pepper
- ½ cup chickpea flour
- 1 tsp garlic powder
- ½ tsp onion powder
- ¼ tsp smoked paprika
- ¼ tsp cayenne pepper
- 2 large eggs
- 1 tbsp whole milk
- 1 ½ cups panko breadcrumbs
- 1 cup canola oil

DIRECTIONS:

1. Season the tomato slices with fine salt and ground black pepper.

2. In a medium mixing bowl, add the chickpea flour, garlic powder, onion powder, smoked paprika and cayenne pepper, and mix to combine. In another mixing bowl, add the eggs and milk, and whisk until foamy. Place the breadcrumbs in a third bowl.

3. Coat the tomato slices in the flour mixture, then the egg mixture, and allow excess liquid to drip off. Coat the tomato slices in the breadcrumbs and press the breadcrumbs carefully into each tomato slice.

4. Heat the canola oil in a large heavy bottom pan over medium heat until hot.

5. Fry the crumbed tomatoes in batches for 1 to 2 minutes, or until the breading starts to turn golden brown. Flip, and cook for an additional 1 to 2 minutes.

6. Transfer the fried tomato slices onto a paper, towel-lined plate to cool and set. Serve warm.

MUSTARD YOGURT CABBAGE

PREP TIME: 10 MIN | SERVES: 4-6

INGREDIENTS:

- ½ (14 oz) bag shredded cabbage
- 1 large apple, peeled, cored, and diced
- 2 cups baby spinach, chopped
- 1 medium carrot, peeled and shredded
- 8 tbsp plain Greek yogurt
- 1 tbsp whole-grain mustard
- 1 tsp granulated sugar
- 1 tsp olive oil
- 1 tsp apple cider vinegar
- 1 tsp lime juice
- Pinch fine salt

DIRECTIONS:

1. In a large mixing bowl, add the shredded cabbage, diced apple, chopped spinach and shredded carrot, and toss to combine.

2. In a small mixing bowl, add the Greek yogurt, whole-grain mustard, granulated sugar, olive oil, apple cider vinegar, lime juice, and fine salt, and whisk to combine.

3. Drizzle the yogurt sauce over the cabbage mixture and mix to combine. Serve immediately or allow it to chill in the refrigerator until serving.

ROSEMARY POTATOES

COOK TIME: 1 HOUR | SERVES: 6

INGREDIENTS:

- Non-stick cooking spray
- ¼ cup canola oil
- 2 tsp fine salt
- ¼ tsp ground black pepper
- 2 tbsp garlic, minced
- 2 tbsp rosemary, sprigs removed and finely chopped
- 3 lb. small red potatoes, peeled and cut in half

DIRECTIONS:

1. Preheat oven to 400°F or 200°C. Line a baking pan with aluminum foil and coat with cooking spray.

2. In a large mixing bowl, add the canola oil, fine salt, ground black pepper, minced garlic and chopped rosemary, and whisk to combine. Add the cut potatoes and toss to coat.

3. Transfer the potatoes onto the prepared pan and spread them out into one layer. Roast in the oven for 45 minutes to 1 hour until browned and crisp.

BALSAMIC BROCCOLI

COOK TIME: 30 MIN | SERVES: 4

INGREDIENTS:

- Non-stick cooking spray
- ¼ cup olive oil
- 1 tsp fine salt
- ¼ tsp ground black pepper
- 1-2 heads of broccoli, cut into florets
- 1 tbsp balsamic vinegar
- 2 tbsp maple syrup

DIRECTIONS:

1. Preheat the oven to 400°F or 200°C. Line a baking pan with aluminum foil and coat with cooking spray.

2. In a large bowl, add the olive oil, fine salt and ground black pepper, and mix to combine. Add the broccoli florets and toss to coat.

3. Place the broccoli on the baking pan and roast for 20 to 30 minutes until tender and browned. Remove from the oven.

4. In a large bowl, add the balsamic vinegar and maple syrup, and whisk to combine. Add the roasted broccoli and toss to cover. Serve warm.

SWEET & SOUR SAUCE

COOK TIME: 6 MIN | MAKES: 1 CUP

INGREDIENTS:

- ½ cup rice vinegar
- ½ cup water
- ½ cup granulated sugar
- 3 tbsp gluten-free oyster sauce
- 1 tsp garlic, minced
- 3 tsp red pepper flakes
- 1 ½ tbsp cornstarch

DIRECTIONS:

1. In a small stockpot over medium heat, add the rice vinegar, water, granulated sugar, oyster sauce, minced garlic and red pepper flakes, and mix to combine. Allow to simmer and cook for 5 minutes.
2. In a glass measuring jug, add 2 tablespoons of the vinegar liquid and the cornstarch, and whisk to combine, making sure there are no lumps.
3. Whisk the cornstarch slurry back into the pot and cook for 1 to 2 minutes, whisking continuously until the sauce thickens. Serve hot or cold.

HONEY & MUSTARD SAUCE

COOK TIME: 12 MIN | MAKES: 2 CUPS

INGREDIENTS:

- 1 tbsp olive oil
- 1 brown onion, minced
- 1 tbsp garlic, minced
- ¼ cup honey
- 1 (15oz) can tomato sauce
- 2 tsp smoked paprika
- 1 tsp ground cumin
- 3 tsp whole-grain mustard
- 1 tbsp balsamic vinegar

DIRECTIONS:

1. In a small stockpot over medium heat, add the olive oil until hot.
2. Add the minced onion and minced garlic, and cook for 5 minutes until softened.
3. Add the honey and cook for 2 minutes more.
4. Add the tomato sauce, smoked paprika, ground cumin, whole-grain mustard and balsamic vinegar, and whisk to combine. Allow to simmer for 5 minutes and serve with your choice of meat.

TURMERIC SWEET POTATO

COOK TIME: 40 MIN | SERVES: 4

INGREDIENTS:

- 2 large sweet potatoes, cut into spears
- 4 tsp canola oil
- ¼ tsp garlic salt
- ½ tsp ground turmeric
- ¼ tsp garlic powder

DIRECTIONS:

1. Preheat the oven to 400°F or 200°C.

2. Lay the sweet potatoes spears on a large baking pan. Drizzle the canola oil over the potatoes and use a basting brush to coat them.

3. Sprinkle the garlic salt, ground turmeric and garlic powder over the potato spears, and use the same brush to fully coat the potatoes in the seasoning.

4. Bake for 40 minutes, flipping halfway, through the baking. Turn the oven to broil and cook for a few extra minutes for crispy fries.

Tip: you can replace the sweet potatoes with russet potatoes and serve with the honey & mustard sauce.

SWISS CHEESE BEANS

COOK TIME: 10 MIN | SERVES: 4

INGREDIENTS:

- 1 lb. fresh green beans, ends trimmed
- ¼ cup water
- 2 tsp canola oil
- ¼ tsp ground black pepper
- 1/3 cup Swiss cheese, shredded
- 1/3 cup sliced almonds, toasted

DIRECTIONS:

1. In a large heavy bottom pan over medium heat, add the trimmed green beans and water, cover, and cook for 2 to 4 minutes. Uncover and continue cooking for 4 minutes, stirring occasionally until the water has evaporated. Remove from the heat and add the canola oil.

2. While still hot, sprinkle the ground black pepper, shredded Swiss cheese, and sliced almonds, and mix to combine. Serve immediately.

MAPLE-GLAZED CARROTS

COOK TIME: 20 MIN | SERVES: 4

INGREDIENTS:

- 16 oz bag carrot chips
- 2 tbsp unsalted butter
- 2 tbsp maple syrup
- 1 tbsp lime juice
- ¼ tsp fine salt
- 2 tsp dried sage

DIRECTIONS:

1. In a medium-sized stockpot, bring water to a boil over high heat.
2. Add the carrot chips and cook for 10 to 15 minutes until tender. Drain the carrots and add them back into the pan. Add the unsalted butter, maple syrup and lime juice, and mix to combine.
3. Cook for 5 minutes, or until the glaze coats the carrots. Season with fine salt and dried sage. Serve warm.

GARLIC & THYME CORN

COOK TIME: 40 MIN | SERVES: 6

INGREDIENTS:

- 6 sweet corns on the cob
- ¼ cup unsalted butter
- 1 tsp garlic, minced
- 1 tsp fresh thyme, sprigs removed
- ½ teaspoon fine salt

DIRECTIONS:

1. Preheat the oven to 375°F or 190°C.
2. Place the whole corn cobs on a rimmed baking pan. Bake for 40 minutes.
3. In a microwave-safe bowl, add the unsalted butter, minced garlic, thyme, and fine salt. Microwave for 20 seconds, or until the butter has melted.
4. Remove the corn from the oven and place them onto serving plates. Using a basting brush, brush the melted butter mixture over the corn and serve.

Tip: you can use frozen, whole kernel corn in place of the cob. Drizzle the butter mixture over the roasted whole kernel just before serving.

CHEESE SAUCE

COOK TIME: 4 MIN | MAKES: 2 CUPS

INGREDIENTS:

- 3 tbsp unsalted butter
- 3 tbsp Bob's Red Mill gluten-free 1-to-1 baking flour
- 2 cups whole milk
- Fine salt
- Ground black pepper
- 1 cup sharp cheddar cheese, shredded

DIRECTIONS:

1. In a medium-sized stockpot over high heat, add the unsalted butter and cook until melted and sizzling.

2. Reduce the heat to medium and remove the pot from the heat. Add the flour and whisk to combine and no lumps remain. Cook for 2 minutes, or longer for a deeper roux.

3. Add the whole milk 1/4 cup at a time, whisking vigorously after each addition. Place the pot back onto the heat and cook for 2 minutes, whisking continuously until thickened. Do not boil.

4. Remove from the heat and season with fine salt and ground black pepper. Add the shredded cheddar cheese and whisk until melted.

CUCUMBER & DILL SAUCE

PREP TIME: 5 MIN | SERVES: 8

INGREDIENTS:

- ½ cup lite mayonnaise or plain Greek yogurt
- 2 tbsp fresh dill, finely chopped
- 1 mini cucumber, cut lengthwise, seeds removed and finely diced
- 1 tsp lemon juice
- ¼ tsp garlic salt

DIRECTIONS:

1. In a small mixing bowl with a lid, add the lite mayonnaise or Greek yogurt, chopped dill, diced cucumber, lemon juice and garlic salt, and mix to combine.

2. Cover with the lid and chill in the refrigerator for 30 minutes before serving.

COOKIES, TARTS & CAKES

STRAWBERRY CHEESECAKE

PREP TIME: 5 MIN | SERVES: 9

INGREDIENTS:

- 2 cups gluten-free graham crackers
- ½ cup unsalted butter, melted
- 2 (8 oz) packages smooth cream cheese, at room temperature
- 1 cup sour cream
- 1 cup powdered sugar
- 1 tsp vanilla extract
- 1 (15 oz) can Lucky Leaf strawberry pie filling

DIRECTIONS:

1. In a food processor, pulse the graham crackers until finely ground. Add the melted unsalted butter and pulse until well combined.

2. Transfer the mixture into an 8-by-8-inch round baking dish and press down with the back of a flat-bottomed cup. Place in the freezer for 5 minutes.

3. In the bowl of a stand mixer, add the cream cheese, sour cream, powdered sugar and vanilla extract, and beat on high speed until smooth.

4. Spread the cream cheese mixture over the chilled crust. Return to the freezer for 15 minutes.

5. Pour the strawberry pie filling over the top of the cheesecake, and gently spread to cover the top. Refrigerate until ready to serve.

STRAWBERRY MACAROONS

COOK TIME: 20 MIN | MAKES: 24

INGREDIENTS:

- 2 large egg whites
- Pinch fine salt
- ¼ cup granulated sugar
- ¼ tsp strawberry extract
- 2 cups unsweetened shredded coconut

DIRECTIONS:

1. Preheat the oven to 325°F or 170°C. Line a rimmed baking pan with parchment paper.

2. Using a hand mixer, in a medium mixing bowl, add the egg whites and fine salt, and beat until soft peaks form.

3. Beat the granulated sugar 1 tablespoon at a time for 1 minute until the egg whites are thick and glossy. Add the strawberry extract and beat until incorporated.

4. Fold in the shredded coconut until just combined. Refrigerate for 20 minutes.

5. Using a dessert spoon, scoop the batter and drop the portions onto the prepared baking sheet in neat mounds.

6. Bake for 20 minutes, or until beginning to brown. Cool before serving.

Tip: if the macaroon batter is spreading on the baking pan, return the batter to the refrigerator and allow it to chill for a longer time.

CHOCOMINT COOKIES

COOK TIME: 10 MIN | MAKES: 60

INGREDIENTS:

- 1 cup Bob's Red Mill gluten-free 1-to-1 baking flour, plus more for dusting
- ½ cup unsweetened cocoa powder
- ½ tsp baking powder
- ½ tsp baking soda
- ¼ tsp fine salt

- 5 tbsp unsalted butter, room temperature
- ¾ cup granulated sugar
- 1 large egg, room temperature,
- 1 large egg yolk, room temperature
- 2 tsp peppermint extract, divided
- 18 oz dark chocolate chips

DIRECTIONS:

1. In a large mixing bowl, add the flour, unsweetened cocoa powder, baking powder, baking soda, and fine salt. Whisk to combine.

2. In the bowl of a stand mixer, beat the unsalted butter and granulated sugar for 1 to 3 minutes on high speed until well combined and lighter in color.

3. Add the large egg and mix to incorporate. Add the large egg yolk and mix well again.

4. Add 1½ teaspoons of peppermint extract, and beat for 1 to 2 minutes until fully combined.

5. Reduce the speed to low and add the flour mixture, beat to combine. The dough will be very thick a sticky.

6. Transfer the dough onto plastic wrap and cover loosely. Refrigerate for 1 hour, or overnight.

7. On a clean, floured surface, roll the dough to a large circle, about 1/8 inch thick. Use a round cookie cutter to cut out the dough and place the cookies on a baking pan lined with parchment paper. Refrigerate for 15 to 30 minutes.

8. Preheat the oven to 350°F or 180°C. Bake for 12 to 15 minutes and allow the cookies to cool completely.

9. Heat a small stockpot filled halfway with water and place a heat-resistant bowl on top. Do not allow the water to boil.

10. Add the dark chocolate chips into the bowl and allow them to melt, making sure no moisture falls into the chocolate.

11. Once the chocolate has melted, add the remaining ½ teaspoon peppermint extract and mix to incorporate.

12. Use a fork to dip each cookie into the melted mint chocolate until completely covered. Allow the excess chocolate to drip off, and scrape the bottom of each cookie with another fork before setting the cookie on a fresh piece of parchment paper to harden. Let the cookies cool and harden before serving.

Tip: for the chocolate to harden faster, place them in the refrigerator or freezer for a few minutes.

CHEWY COFFEE COOKIES

COOK TIME: 15 MIN | MAKES: 12

INGREDIENTS:

- ½ cup unsalted butter, melted
- ½ cup light brown sugar
- ⅓ cup granulated sugar
- 1 large egg
- 1½ tsp coffee extract or vanilla extract
- 1 ⅓ cups Bob's Red Mill gluten-free 1-to-1 baking flour
- ¼ cup potato starch
- ½ tsp baking soda
- ½ tsp fine salt
- 1 ⅓ cups white chocolate chips

DIRECTIONS:

1. In the bowl of a stand mixer, add the melted butter, light brown sugar, granulated sugar, egg and coffee or vanilla extract, and beat on high until smooth.

2. In a medium mixing bowl, add the flour, potato starch, baking soda and fine salt, and whisk to combine. Pour one-third of the flour mixture into the bowl with the wet ingredients and beat on medium speed until smooth. Repeat with the remaining flour mixture and beat until a smooth dough forms. Fold in the white chocolate chips.

3. Cover the bowl with plastic wrap and refrigerate for 1 hour. In the last 10 minutes of chilling, preheat the oven to 350°F or 180°C and line a baking pan with parchment paper.

4. Split the dough into 12 equal pieces and roll each piece in your hands to form a ball.

5. Place the balls on the lined baking pan, making sure to leave space between each.

6. Bake for 14 to 16 minutes, or until the edges are golden and the centers have risen. Allow them to cool on the baking pan for 5 to 8 minutes before transferring onto a cool rack.

Tip: if the dough becomes too soft, place it back into the refrigerator to chill.

PECAN NUT COOKIES

COOK TIME: 15 MIN | MAKES: 24

INGREDIENTS:

- 1 ¾ cups Bob's Red Mill gluten-free 1-to-1 baking flour
- 1 tsp baking soda
- ¾ tsp xanthan gum
- ½ tsp fine salt
- 8 tbsp unsalted butter, melted and cooled
- ¾ cup light brown sugar
- ⅓ cup granulated sugar
- 1 large egg
- 2 tbsp whole milk
- 1 tbsp vanilla extract
- ¾ cup dark chocolate chips
- ½ cup pecan nuts, chopped

DIRECTIONS:

1. In a large mixing bowl, add the flour, baking soda, xanthan gum, and fine salt whisk to combine. Set aside.

2. In another large mixing bowl, add the melted butter, light brown sugar, and granulated sugar, and whisk until no lumps remain.

3. Add the egg, whole milk and vanilla extract, and whisk until smooth. Add the flour mixture and mix until a sticky dough is formed. Fold in the dark chocolate chips and chopped pecan nuts. Cover the bowl with plastic wrap and let the dough rest for 30 minutes.

4. Preheat the oven to 350°F or 180°C. Line 2 baking pans with parchment paper. Using 2 dessert spoons, portion out the dough and space 2 inches apart on prepared sheets.

5. Bake the cookies for 12 to 14 minutes until golden brown.

6. Allow the cookies to cool on the pan for 5 minutes, then transfer to the wire rack.

GINGER COOKIES

COOK TIME: 25 MIN | MAKES: 30

INGREDIENTS:

- 6 tbsp canola oil
- ¾ cup packed dark brown sugar
- 1 tbsp fresh ginger, grated
- 1 tbsp ground ginger
- ½ tsp ground cinnamon
- ½ tsp ground allspice
- ⅛ tsp ground black pepper
- 1 ⅓ cups Bob's Red Mill gluten-free 1-to-1 baking flour
- 1 tsp baking powder
- ¼ tsp baking soda
- ¼ tsp xanthan gum
- ¼ tsp fine salt
- 1 large egg
- ½ cup granulated sugar

DIRECTIONS:

1. In the bowl of a stand mixer, add the canola oil, dark brown sugar, grated ginger, ground ginger, ground cinnamon, ground allspice, and ground black pepper, and beat on high speed until smooth.

2. In another mixing bowl, add the flour, baking powder, baking soda, xanthan gum and fine salt, and mix to combine.

3. Beat the egg into the butter-spice mixture until well combined. Add several tablespoons of the flour mixture at a time, beating after each addition until a sticky dough forms. Cover the bowl with plastic wrap and let the dough rest for 30 minutes.

4. Preheat the oven to 300°F or 150°C. Line 2 baking pans with parchment paper. Place the granulated sugar in a shallow dish.

5. Working with 2 teaspoons of dough at a time, roll the dough into balls and drop it into the sugar. Coat each dough ball with sugar and space them 1½ inches apart on the prepared pans.

6. Bake the cookies for 20 to 25 minutes until the cookies are set.

7. Allow the cookies to cool on the pans for 5 minutes, then transfer to the wire rack. Cool completely before serving.

WALNUT BROWNIES

COOK TIME: 35 MIN | SERVES: 9

INGREDIENTS:

- Non-stick cooking spray
- ½ cup unsalted butter, melted
- 1 tbsp vanilla extract
- ¾ cup granulated sugar
- ½ cup light brown sugar
- 2 large eggs, room temperature
- ¾ cup Bob's Red Mill gluten-free 1-to-1 baking flour
- ⅛ tsp xanthan gum
- ½ cup unsweetened cocoa powder
- ½ tsp baking soda
- ½ tsp fine salt
- ½ cup walnuts, roughly chopped and divided

DIRECTIONS:

1. Preheat the oven to 350°F or 180°C. Line a deep baking pan with parchment paper and spray the bottom and sides with non-stick cooking spray.

2. In the bowl of a stand mixer, add the unsalted, vanilla extract, granulated sugar and light brown sugar, and beat until fully combined.

3. Add the eggs one at a time, beating after each addition until fully combined.

4. In a medium mixing bowl, add the gluten-free flour, xanthan gum, unsweetened cocoa powder, baking soda and fine salt, and mix to combine.

5. With the mixer on low, add the flour mixture several tablespoons at a time into the butter mixture and beat until fully combined and smooth. Fold in a ¼ cup of chopped walnuts.

6. Pour the batter into the prepared baking pan and sprinkle the remaining ¼ cup chopped walnuts on top.

7. Bake for 30 to 35 minutes or until a toothpick inserted comes out barely clean and the sides start to pull away from the pan. Allow the brownies to cool for 30 minutes in the pan before slicing.

Tip: for an extra chocolate flavor, melt some dark chocolate chips and drizzle it over the cooled brownies and serve.

PINEAPPLE BUTTER CAKE

COOK TIME: 55 MIN | SERVES: 9

INGREDIENTS:

Topping
- Non-stick cooking spray
- ¼ cup unsalted butter, melted
- 2/3 cup light brown sugar
- 1 (20 oz) can sliced pineapple, drained
- 9 maraschino cherries, stems removed

Cake
- ⅓ cup unsalted butter
- 1 cup granulated sugar
- 1 tsp vanilla extract
- 1 large egg
- 1 ⅓ cups Bob's Red Mill gluten-free 1-to-1 baking flour
- ½ tsp xanthan gum
- 1 ½ tsp baking powder
- ½ tsp fine salt
- 1 cup unsweetened cashew milk

DIRECTIONS:

For the topping:

1. Preheat the oven to 350°F or 180°C. Coat a round cake pan with non-stick cooking spray.

2. Pour the melted butter into the pan and sprinkle the light brown sugar over the butter. Place the pineapple slices on top of the brown sugar and then place a cherry in the center of each pineapple slice.

For the cake:

1. In the bowl of a stand mixer, add the butter and granulated sugar and beat until lighter in color. Add the vanilla extract and egg, and beat until fully combined.

2. Add the flour, xanthan gum, baking powder and fine salt, and beat until well incorporated. Add the cashew milk and beat for 2 minutes on medium speed until smooth.

3. Pour the cake batter over the pineapples in the pan. Bake for 50 to 55 minutes or until a toothpick inserted comes out clean. Allow the cake to cool for 10 minutes, then invert the cake onto a serving plate and serve warm.

BERRY MEDLEY CRUMBLE

COOK TIME: 25 MIN | SERVES: 6

INGREDIENTS:

- 5 tbsp palm oil shortening, divided
- 6 cups whole berry medley, thawed and strained
- 6 tbsp granulated sugar, divided
- 3 tbsp tapioca flour (starch)
- 1 cup whole-grain gluten-free flour blend
- ¼ tsp fine salt

DIRECTIONS:

1. Preheat the oven to 350°F or 180°C.

2. Coat the inside of a deep casserole dish with 1 tablespoon of shortening.

3. Add the strained berry medley to the prepared dish and top with 2 tablespoons of granulated sugar and tapioca flour. Gently toss to coat.

4. In a medium mixing bowl, add the remaining 4 tablespoons shortening, the remaining 4 tablespoons granulated sugar, the flour blend, and fine salt. Mix with your hands and then crumble it over the berries.

5. Bake for 25 minutes, or until the top is golden brown and the berries are bubbling. Allow to cool for 10 minutes before serving.

Tip: whip up 1 cup of fresh whipping cream and serve it on the side, or 1 scoop of vanilla ice cream.

COURGETTE CACAO CAKE

COOK TIME: 25 MIN | SERVES: 8

INGREDIENTS:

- 5 tbsp unsalted butter, at room temperature, divided
- ½ cup light brown sugar
- 4 large eggs
- 1 tbsp vanilla extract
- 1 cup finely ground blanched almond flour
- 1 tbsp coconut flour
- ½ cup unsweetened cocoa powder
- 1 tsp baking soda
- ½ tsp fine salt
- 1 cup courgette, shredded

DIRECTIONS:

1. Preheat the oven to 325°F or 170°C. Coat the inside of a cake pan with 1 tablespoon of butter. Line the pan with parchment paper.

2. In the bowl of a stand mixer, add the light brown sugar and the remaining 4 tablespoons of butter, and beat for 1 minute until lighter in color.

3. Add the eggs and vanilla extract, and beat for 1 minute until incorporated.

4. In a large mixing bowl, sift in the almond flour, coconut flour, unsweetened cocoa powder, baking soda and fine salt, and mix to combine.

5. Squeeze the excess moisture from the courgettes with your hands and then fold it into the cake batter.

6. Pour the batter into the prepared pan. Bake for 20 to 25 minutes, or until a toothpick inserted comes out clean. Allow to cool for 10 minutes in the pan before removing it and placing the cake on a wire rack to cool completely.

FROSTED CARROT CUPCAKES

COOK TIME: 20 MIN | MAKES: 12

INGREDIENTS:

For the frosting
- ½ cup unsalted butter, room temperature
- 8 oz Philadelphia original cream cheese brick, room temperature
- 1 tsp vanilla extract
- ¼ tsp fine salt
- 4 cups powdered sugar

For the cake
- 1 cup almond flour
- 1 cup coconut flour
- 2 tbsp xanthan gum
- 1 tbsp baking powder
- ½ tbsp baking soda
- 1 ½ tsp ground cinnamon
- 1 cup granulated sugar
- ¾ cup canola oil
- 3 tbsp unsalted butter
- 2 large eggs
- ½ cup water
- 1 tbsp vanilla extract
- 3 cups carrots, peeled, and finely grated

DIRECTIONS:

For the frosting:
1. In the bowl of a stand mixer, add the unsalted butter and cream cheese, beat on high speed for 2 minutes, or until creamy and no lumps remain.
2. Add the vanilla extract and fine salt, and beat until combined.
3. With the mixer on low speed, add several tablespoons of the powdered sugar at a time, beating after each addition, and all the sugar has been incorporated.
4. Transfer the frosting into a bowl, cover with plastic wrap, and refrigerate until ready to use.

For the cake:
1. Preheat the oven to 350°F or 180°C. Line a muffin tin with muffin liners, and set aside.
2. In a large mixing bowl, add the almond flour, coconut flour, xanthan gum, baking powder, baking soda, and ground cinnamon, and mix to combine.
3. In a clean stand mixer bowl, add the granulated sugar, canola oil, butter, eggs, water and vanilla extract, and beat on high speed to combine. Add the grated carrots and beat again.
4. With the mixer on low speed, combine the flour mixture with the wet ingredients and beat for 1 minute until fully incorporated.
5. Fill each muffin cup to the brim with batter and bake for 20 to 22 minutes, or until the tops are golden brown and a toothpick inserted comes out clean.
6. Allow to cool completely before frosting.

Tip: use a cake decorating piping bag with an open star piping nozzle for the frosting. Alternately, you can use a spoon or straight stainless-steel spatula to cover the tops with frosting.

MICROWAVE CHERRY CAKE

COOK TIME: 1 MIN | SERVES: 2

INGREDIENTS:

- 2 tbsp coconut flour
- 2 tbsp almond flour
- 1 tbsp granulated sugar
- ½ tsp baking powder
- Pinch fine salt
- ¼ cup unsweetened cashew milk
- 1 large egg, beaten
- ¼ tsp cherry extract
- 1 cup fresh cherries, pitted, stems removed and halved for garnish
- Vanilla ice cream, for garnish

DIRECTIONS:

1. In a medium mixing bowl, add the coconut flour, almond flour, granulated sugar, baking powder and fine salt, and whisk to combine.

2. Add the almond milk, beaten egg and cherry extract, and whisk to combine. Allow the batter to sit for 5 minutes.

3. Divide the batter into 2 coffee mugs. One mug at a time, microwave for 1 minute.

4. Let it cool for 5 minutes. Serve warm with halved cherries and vanilla ice cream on top.

ITALIAN COOKIES

COOK TIME: 15 MIN | MAKES: 18

INGREDIENTS:

- 1 ⅔ cups slivered almonds
- 1 ⅓ cups granulated sugar
- 2 large egg whites
- 1 cup pine nuts

DIRECTIONS:

1. Preheat the oven to 375°F or 190°C. Line 2 baking pans with parchment paper.

2. In a food processor, add the slivered almonds and granulated sugar, and process for 30 seconds, or until finely ground. Add the egg whites and process for 30 seconds until a smooth dough is formed. Transfer the mixture into a bowl. Place the pine nuts in a shallow dish.

3. Working with 1 tablespoon of dough at a time, roll into balls, then roll the dough in pine nuts to coat, and space evenly apart on prepared pans.

4. Bake for 13 to 15 minutes until light golden brown. Allow the cookies to cool on the pans for 5 minutes, then transfer onto a wire rack to cool completely.

LIME MADELEINES

COOK TIME: 10 MIN | MAKES: 12

INGREDIENTS:

- ⅓ cup plus ¼ cup Bob's Red Mill gluten-free 1-to-1 baking flour
- ¼ tsp baking powder
- ⅛ tsp fine salt
- 1 large egg
- 2 large yolks
- 6 tbsp granulated sugar
- 4 tbsp unsalted butter, melted and cooled
- 1 tbsp lime zest, grated
- 1 tsp lime extract
- Non-stick cooking spray
- Powdered sugar

DIRECTIONS:

1. In a medium mixing bowl, add the flour, baking powder and fine salt, and whisk to combine.

2. In a large mixing bowl, add the whole egg, egg yolks, granulated sugar, melted butter, lime zest and lime extract, and whisk until smooth.

3. Fold the flour mixture into the wet ingredients for 1 minute, or until the flour is completely incorporated. Cover the bowl with plastic wrap and let the batter rest for 20 minutes.

4. Preheat the oven to 375°F or 190°C. Coat a silicone madeleine pan with non-stick cooking spray and set the silicone mole in a rimmed baking pan.

5. Working with 2 teaspoons of batter at a time, portion the batter into the molds. Bake the madeleines for 8 to 10 minutes until the edges begin to brown and spring back when pressed lightly.

6. Allow to cool for 5 minutes. Pop the madeleines out of the mold and place them on a wire rack, ridged side up to cool completely.

7. Dust the madeleines with powdered sugar before serving.

VANILLA & BANANA CUPCAKES

COOK TIME: 20 MIN | MAKES: 24

INGREDIENTS:

Cupcakes
- ½ cup unsweetened almond milk
- 2 tsp white vinegar
- ¼ cup unsalted butter
- 1 ½ cups granulated sugar
- ½ tsp vanilla extract
- 3 large eggs
- 1 ½ cups Bob's Red Mill gluten-free 1-to-1 baking flour
- ½ tsp xanthan gum

- 1 ½ tsp baking powder
- ½ tsp fine salt
- 3 medium ripe bananas, mashed

Banana Buttercream
- 1 cup unsalted butter, softened
- 1 small ripe banana, mashed
- ¼ tsp lemon juice
- ¼ tsp banana or vanilla extract
- 3 cups powdered sugar

DIRECTIONS:

Cupcake:

1. Preheat the oven to 350°F or 180°C. Line two cupcake pans with baking cup liners.

2. In a small mixing bowl, add the almond milk and vinegar and allow it to sit for 5 minutes until curdled.

3. In the bowl of a stand mixer, add the butter and granulated sugar, and beat until lighter in color. Add the vanilla extract and beat again. Add the eggs one at a time and beat after each addition until fully combined.

4. In a medium mixing bowl, add the flour, baking powder, and fine salt. Add the flour mixture into the butter mixture and beat until combined. Add the mashed banana and the curdled milk mixture to batter and beat until combined.

5. Spoon the batter into the prepared cupcake tins. Bake for 18 to 20 minutes or until a cake tester inserted comes out clean. Remove the cupcakes and place on a wire rack to cool completely.

Banana Buttercream:

1. In a clean stand mixer bowl, add the butter, and beat until smooth, scraping down the sides of the bowl.

2. Add the mashed banana, lemon juice, and banana or vanilla extract and beat until fully combined. Scrape down the sides of the bowl.

3. Add the powdered sugar 1 cup at a time, beating after each addition and the buttercream is firm. Refrigerate the frosting for 5 minutes before spreading on top of the cupcakes.

Tip: add more powdered sugar into the buttercream mixture if you find that the buttercream is too soft. Use butter that has a minimal amount of water, or else the buttercream will split.

Printed in the USA
CPSIA information can be obtained
at www.ICGtesting.com
LVHW081036201023
761326LV00086B/95

9 781922 590329